New Venture
Methodology

New Venture Methodology

Donald H. Slocum

AMERICAN MANAGEMENT ASSOCIATION

International standard book number: 0-8144-5297-3
Library of Congress catalog card number: 78-188845
First printing

To
Those Fellow Workers
Whose Venture Spirit
Supplied the Inspiration

Preface

MUCH attention has been given to new ventures and venture management over the past several years. Many corporations have assembled groups to carry out the function. Nor has there been any absence of individual entrepreneurs venturing into businesses with concepts which they hope the market will accept. The guidelines for new ventures were never clearly defined, and the basis appeared to be some articles on venturing in diverse journals, with each article covering some portion of the process from planning it to managing it.

Venture groups and various business development groups whose charter was to locate and initiate new ventures have not been uniformly successful. Part of the problem can be traced to the methods used. Obviously one can look to several individuals or some select companies and see that new venture methodology works when properly applied. Theory frequently encumbers the operation and results in an emphasis on mechanization rather than on productivity. A pragmatic view can be taken that offers for the first time a rather detailed method that is both flexible and workable.

The venture analyst, the manager, the entrepreneur, and the chief operating officer of a company must come to grips with the problem of business expansion and diversification through the use of available resources. In no case are the alternatives easily distinguishable from one another by a superficial look or intuitive judgments. The risk is too high, the need too great, and the rewards too desirable or necessary to justify a haphazard approach to new business development.

While there is no one way to venture, this text presents a composite of the elements needed for success. The tools are described in broad terms, allowing appropriate tailoring for the individual entrepreneur or the large company with extensive peripheral services. The key of practical business planning opens the gate, but only proper implementation supplies the motivating force that carries the business through to a panorama of profitable markets.

Donald H. Slocum

Contents

1

Introduction

THROUGHOUT the sixties, the development and introductory marketing of new products proceeded at an unprecedented pace. With little resistance from customers or competition, costs were apparently of secondary concern, and many companies both small and large seemed to measure dominance in the marketplace in terms of the quantity of entries rather than long-term successes of new products. The paramount philosophy was that everything in business moves so rapidly that immediate participation in the market is necessary for the vitality of a company, regardless of potential adverse consequences. This general attitude had many exceptions, however, and not every product or market entry was taken lightly in terms of corporate effort, costs, and profits.

During this time, a body of knowledge contributing to a better understanding of the intricate world of technology and new-product market entries was growing. This knowledge, however, was not given priority use because of the optimistic economic climate. The more new products were introduced, the clearer it became that many were unsuccessful. These failures caused great stress on company budgets, which were beginning to show the strain of increased costs and lower profits despite improved sales pictures. And so a growing number of companies began to give attention to making appropriate choices of new market entries.

This focus on selection of proper new products and markets was not the only change, for the choice was dependent upon numerous other factors, to be discussed in this text. It did, however, demonstrate the need for not only tools of evaluation but a method that

1

would circumvent some of the difficulties inherent in taking commercial advantage of new business opportunities. As the pendulum swung, so did caution over new-product development and introduction. Overcautious management demanded greater assurance of low risk before committing funds. Superimposed on this state of affairs was the diversification most companies were attempting, made possible by the acquisition of technology, in their desire for improved growth rates. In addition, their reluctance to move too aggressively, the enormous difficulties of effecting growth in a conservative business climate, the newness of areas of interest to a given company, and the number of people required to make decisions resulted in an awareness that a new procedure was needed to attack the problem. Companies that recognized this change and adopted a new methodology are now regarded as leaders, not only in their respective fields but in the realm of management techniques.

The purpose of this book is to define and demonstrate the methodology that has grown from this historical need, which we call *New Venture Methodology*. It is a technique designed to rapidly convert ideas, inventions, innovations, and improvements into viable and profitable undertakings. It is a pragmatic approach that encompasses all the tools available to modern corporations today, including the effective utilization of procedures that have been previously misused or that have recently grown out of theory and practice in companies of all sizes.

Special application of New Venture Methodology to small companies or small organizations within larger corporate frameworks is emphasized. Entrepreneurs who operate new ventures often use a small-business approach, which has an individual appeal and many inherent cost savings. This book recommends, however, that these and other methods developed from theory and now in practice be used in a more intense, compact, and efficient manner.

New Venture Methodology draws upon the key factors, roles, and basic elements of these specific uses and interweaves them in a system of priorities for devising a step-by-step procedure ideally suited for developing new market entries or new business opportunities. It has the flexibility to be tailored to businesses of any size. Its goal is to present the most economical, time-saving, and market-oriented method for turning a concept into a profit-producing operation with minimal cost and risk. It is not cheap to develop new businesses, nor can risk or uncertainty be eliminated; but with this methodology, a corporate body is able to realize some of its growth goals through new businesses and new products.

As firms recognized the problems involved in taking advantage of business opportunities and reassessed the methods used, a new vocabulary developed. Phraseology in itself cannot supply solutions to the problem of converting concepts into business. But terms are important to us for a better understanding of mechanisms and of variations within a method as it applies to various situations. In general usage, the words *idea, invention, innovation, improvement,* and *opportunity* are frequently interchangeable. But as they are used in the new approach to business development, each takes on a separate and distinct meaning.

For instance, *idea* is usually defined as a mental picture, an intention, a plan, a notion. By its very nature it lacks substance, and from a product standpoint it is elementary in the stages of development. Under New Venture Methodology, depending on their maturity and the ease with which they could be translated into something tangible, most ideas would be assigned to a research program. No such program would be initiated, however, unless a business opportunity appeared to be feasible in the future.

Invention—the act of devising, discovering, contriving—is more appropriately handled by the New Venture Methodology. In this case a specific entity exists, in practice as well as in concept. The technical input differs from that required for an idea. It may still be in an early stage of development, so it should be viewed cautiously.

Innovation means a change from established custom or practice, a modification, a new thing. In any of these implications, New Venture Methodology is most appropriate. It is necessary to distinguish, however, between a new product and a change in marketing approach, a new market, or a major product-line modification. The input, analysis, and evaluation must be restructured to meet these various situations.

Improvement relates generally to existing products; however, if the improvement will permit a product's entry into an associated or a new business, New Venture Methodology is readily applied. For example, the technique is effective as the product becomes more sophisticated or as the improvement grossly affects the manufacturing, marketing, or direction of the corporation. The point is that integral parts of New Venture Methodology can be used to determine the value of product improvement, but the function of improving a product or product lines, if not the direct responsibility of the operating group, should be closely tied to it as a business defense to keep ahead of competition.

It is outside the purpose of this text to discuss and interrelate fully the expanded meanings and implications of the words *idea, invention, innovation,* and *improvement.* Several recent publications cover the characteristics of these technical advances in depth. Other writings deal with this subject within different frameworks and frequently relate to the research and development function rather than the business orientation.

All the preceding concepts represent *opportunity.* It is our thesis that all ideas, inventions, innovations, and improvements are opportunities and have some degree of commercial value. The key question, the one this method is designed to answer, is: "Is it right for you?" Opportunity need not rely on the four *I*'s just defined. Imitation with imagination and drive has been and still is a fruitful source of opportunity.

The delineation of both the inherent problems and numerous benefits in New Venture Methodology has led to a more detailed and pragmatic approach to new business. By contrast, conventional reviews of the difficulties encountered in launching new products generally end up in an explanation of why things go wrong, with the words *obstacle, tradition, deterrent,* and *today's business* appearing frequently in these reports.

Rather than attempt to fix the blame or suggest reasons for failure, let us see how one can capitalize on future developments by increasing our attention on the job at hand. It is the goal of the organization as a whole to stay competitive and, whenever possible, to become a leader in the marketplace as well. The two characteristics, although compatible, frequently function independently. Therefore, New Venture Methodology primarily requires that a separate entity, either an individual or an organization, carry out the techniques for successful transition of a new business plan from inception to commercialization. With only one objective, the responsible person or group can measure and be monitored in his or its achievements.

This unidirectionality removes the diluting influence of mundane, day-to-day operations. There are few distractions, and intense effort and interest can therefore be brought to bear by the participants in the group, here called the *venture group.* To carry out such a complex task, multidisciplinary capabilities are needed. The generalist must be competent in recognizing technological advances in the context of a market need, profit incentive in light of production or manufacturing capacity, corporate objectives, fiscal problems, market status, and those myriad details that require imagination, accumulation, coordination, and execution.

We expect from such a multidisciplinary, unidirectional function an independence of action, sanctioned and supported by the highest corporate management. With an intensified market orientation directed toward the goal of putting other concepts into action, the risk is lowered and thorough planning and preparation are increased. The company also gains an expansive technological overview, both internally and externally, along with a business exposure that might otherwise escape its attention.

The primary objective of all this is to find more opportunities, evaluate them more thoroughly, compare them more candidly, and enter markets with an increased chance of success in a shorter time. Hence risk to a company is diminished, and the time required to accomplish a given task is by design dramatically shortened. This time reduction starts to occur as soon as New Venture Methodology is used to initiate action on a new or potential business project. Prior development time, when the first stages of research or engineering are carried out independently of the venture group and before it is absolutely recognized that a venture opportunity exists, is not venture-controlled and cannot be measured as part of the venture operation.

It is essential for the success of New Venture Methodology that the corporation maintain its full support by granting a charter, supplying adequate financing, clearing avenues for entrepreneurship, and providing a small, high-status corporate group of accountable decision makers who can maintain the rapid pace and zealous attitude of the venture group. In the absence of these factors, New Venture Methodology will revert to mere idea and business screening, commercial development, product development, or nonspecific planning that is not action oriented and lacks the independence vital to new venture operations. When decision making has not been delegated directly to the venture group, it is slow, and it cannot reasonably be considered a function of the method. There is an obvious need for decisions to be controlled, if not dominated and made, by the venture group leader. Corporate surveillance is not to be eliminated, but decision making is put in proper perspective. These conditions form the core of New Venture Methodology, a more efficient and expedient avenue to successful new business for the individual entrepreneur and the major corporate body.

The Planning Function

Pₗₐₙₙᵢₙ requires continuous interaction among all components of a new venture operation. It is necessary for each aspect of the methodology to be properly considered before one takes action. This requires a complete, composite plan directly related to the particular portion of the method with which a given analyst is working. In addition to these direct supportive plans, there is a more general area of concern that serves as the basic guide for the entire operation. Both types of plans will be discussed in depth.

Many texts and articles have appeared in past years that cover the various phases of planning in detail. One consideration is that planning is a separate function, to be carried out independently of actual operations. The theoretical writings indicate that this potential science is important to adequate business functioning, that it requires individual and collective thought, and that detailed input information is necessary. The framework is critical but flexible, allowing the strategic aspects to be altered to fit the corporate situation. Long-range planning is the searchlight that illuminates the way of the future, viewed from the present. Analytic approaches to growth and expansion are presented in which comparative studies are made or described and relationships between alternatives can be judged. All these touch on the need for management in supervisory and administrative roles to set the stage for formal planning on a continuous basis. The need is obvious, and the results supply a strong justification for the intense effort required.

Within the corporate structure, a sequence of planning steps can be drawn up to outline a general scheme for the new venture operation. This is more than an exercise in corporate self-analysis, though it can serve to accomplish this quite effectively. It should also be realized that conditions change, requiring alteration in the segments of the sequence that can affect the venture. This should be minimal since the corporate objectives, within some well-defined boundaries, are stable yardsticks developed on a year-to-year basis. Consistent attention by management to the planning function will produce principles that clearly define the purpose of a corporation and ideally lead all employees to persistently seek these objectives.

Destiny Planning

The first step in the sequence of corporate planning involves broad philosophical questions concerned with the long-range future plans of the company. Destiny plans consist of words that flow too readily at times, becoming platitudinous by ordinary standards. This is to be anticipated and should be quite acceptable as a starting point. The counterpart of destiny planning in private life would be a man's concern for his general future or the provision of a good life for his family. The small businessman might think in terms of developing an enterprise that assures him a comfortable living throughout his life and establishes for him a respected role in the community. So the corporation will reflect the general desires of its management as well as the traditions initiated by former corporate leaders.

Although *destiny planning* sounds like a tenuous expression of hopes for the future, it should give direction and set the tenor for people at all levels in the organization to help determine and reinforce their career goals. It stabilizes the company, builds spirit, and establishes the caliber of objectives to be set under more precise circumstances. Such hopes and objectives are not easy to determine, but they do exist, and knowledge of corporate destiny plans underlies succeeding plans and projects.

Character Planning

In the character-planning phase, the venture group first poses certain questions to corporate management (or the president of a smaller company) designed to elicit the standards against which movement toward the stated or understood destiny can be measured. It also serves as a long-range procedural tool. Difficulty arises in setting up the concepts the organization will rely on for guidance. These should remain general in content, yet be specific enough to affect subsequent planning steps. Perhaps the best question to ask at this stage is: "Why do we wish to reach the proposed destination?"

To be pragmatic, statements made at this stage of planning should relate specifically to the character of the business and be consistent with its inherent capabilities. It would be incongruous for a leather-producing company, for instance, to promote the elimination of the use of domesticated animals as a food source. This would apply only if the destiny plan called for eventual elimination of the leather business as well. Were this to be the case, a more positive statement would be advisable if not in fact a requirement.

There are several conceptual areas that business would draw from in this phase of planning. Growth is a popular one. It might not be necessary to spell out the desirability of growth in dollar sales, in profits, in personnel, in plant size, in capacity, in efficiency, in recognition, and in numerous other areas that meet the needs of the business. The company and its programs can be much more effectively directed toward the most desirable goals, however, if these are outlined in a plan.

Progress has also become a hallmark in the industrial and service fields. It overlaps growth in some ways, just as it does other conceptual groupings we will discuss. The contributive, scientific, social, and fiscal attitudes have gained much momentum in their use as corporate concepts. Innovation, which is the least peripheral to new ventures, is central to many stated positions of both small and large operations. It is well known that companies use slogans to support and describe their philosophies. Some of the more familiar ones promise or promote "progress," "better things," reliability ("you can be sure"), "better ideas," and the like. Even these are subject to alteration as the business and social environments change.

Character planning is important because it becomes the foundation for the future by defining internal concepts and thinking at a top corporate level. It can be a source of comfort or challenge. It serves as a constant reminder of why the company is in business and intends to remain in business. It differentiates and clarifies and gives depth and substance to the efforts that have been and will be made.

Policy Planning

Another phase of upper-management planning is a statement of policy for the general purposes and objectives of the company. *Policy* has a negative connotation to many, who interpret it in a restrictive sense. No doubt policy will set boundaries on people and subordinate organizations. Used properly, it also answers some pertinent questions about how the corporate body will function and attain its goals and who will assume the various responsibilities. It can go beyond this to describe the means of measuring goals and scheduling periodic reporting, and in such a case, it is a policy-planning document, not a policy statement. When it becomes voluminous, it is usually operationally oriented, whereas the short, concisely stated policy plan is geared to objectives.

For example, such a plan might determine which one of the vice-presidents in a prepared-foods company might develop business in new cereal products, assuming this to be a desirable objective. The plan directs him as it restricts his counterparts within the company. This statement might further indicate that no product will be considered that does not use materials produced exclusively in the United States. A limitation is then imposed on all management. Because of the strong directional tendencies in policy planning, it is important if not critical to divide into readily identifiable sections those inflexible areas from the flexible, the concrete from the general, the required from the desired.

The outline on the next page shows the planning sequence described thus far. It is the basic, top-management planning document that guides all corporate activities. The more articulate it is, the simpler it is for management to develop and define the corporate objectives.

Corporate Objectives

Corporate objectives must be expressed in clear, detailed principles reflecting the company's destiny plans, character or conceptual plans, and policy plans while demonstrating an obvious difference. These specific guidelines go beyond the philosophical aspects of preceding plans and beyond the limited descriptions found in annual reports. Corporate objectives should be insensitive to isolated events that tend to affect operating plans. They reflect strong qualitative planning in that they are realistic, decision-oriented, and shaped by environment, both internal and external. They can take several forms and have been proposed in many ways by numerous authors.

One format might, for example, be based on the types of businesses and products to serve the markets chosen by management. Here we find an orientation toward the physical aspects of the firm's activities. The method used defines and documents the business

Corporate Documentation of Plans

I. Destiny Plan
   A. Near-term position
   B. Five-year objective
   C. Ten-year development
   D. Corporate philosophy
      1. Independence of individual management
      2. General nature
      3. Basic continuity

II. Character Plan
   A. Reasons for direction
   B. Capabilities of organization
   C. Historical significance
   D. Types of goals
      1. Growth
      2. Progress
      3. Innovation
      4. Contribution
      5. Fiscal aims

III. Policy Plan
   A. Corporation responsibility
   B. Organizational accountability
   C. Definition of interest areas
   D. Time to achieve goals
   E. Available tools

objectives in a descriptive literary form. Another type of approach is less descriptive in words but more specific in financial and mathematical terms; this will be discussed in the next major section of the chapter.

Forward Integration

A prime objective may be the forward integration of raw materials the company currently produces. Forward integration might be characterized as stepping stones to market expansion. The plan would choose appropriate areas where the company could increase the value of its product by carrying it closer to its end use. As the product changes in character, several other modes of change must accompany it. An obvious one is a change in the marketing organization, whether structurally, physically, or incrementally. Expansion in manufacturing, technical support, and service may be required. Statements supporting the primary objective are added. In a smaller operation this may be the extent of the company's stated objectives and will give the entire thrust to its future growth, whereas these points may represent only a small portion of the larger corporation's goals.

Backward Integration

The opposite approach can also be a significant objective. Enlarging operations to include the raw materials or component parts needed for the finished products a firm manufactures can result in increased capabilities as well as profits. But it also might result in little or no sales growth, which could be important if sales growth is an objective of the corporate body. The very fact that these diverse objectives have various effects on dollar flow magnifies the problem with setting objectives of this type before developing precise criteria and guiding concepts.

New-Market Development

In a dynamic business situation, there is always a possibility of tapping available or new markets. Present products must be taken into account, though management should be willing to make minor modifications. There are several ways to achieve this end, each having ramifications in time, personnel, and investment of money.

First, a firm can increase the use of its product or service by old or existing customers. Where the consumer uses multiple sources, a firm can enlarge its share through aggressive salesmanship. This objective should be understood to be a continuous one; but to redefine, reinforce, and restate it in company objectives can inspire initiative in the sales force. Second, determination to attract new customers (or perhaps some of the more recalcitrant old ones) can follow. All this may require increased incentives through an improved product, upgraded service and technical support, or more attractive pricing. The last must be carefully examined since results can be widespread, effecting little change in sales with a penalty in profits.

In another new-market approach, a company could search for volume users of a less pure or less sophisticated product or one with a lower service requirement. The increment in business this produces may be less profitable, but it could effectuate an overall growth in sales and profits by increasing efficiency in the use of manufacturing facilities, marketing organizations, and the invested capital of the corporation.

Either of these routes to new markets could be followed success-fully, but it is crucial for the planning to determine the proper one for the company by clearly spelling out the advantages and probable pit-falls of each.

New-Product Development

The subject of new-product development has been so thoroughly investigated in recent years that there is little to be added from the standpoint of corporate objectives. The risk is well recognized, and the desire to attempt it rises and falls with the business climate. There are three ways to carry out this planning phase. One is to take a customer-oriented approach in which existing products are directed toward new applications. A second is to modify the product to meet the needs of new customers or existing customers in peripheral areas. A third might be to use byproducts that present a disposal problem; locating potential users for byproducts or modifying them to a form attractive and appropriate for sale. These three possibilities can be defined in the planning document covering specific objectives.

New-Business Development

The alternative to these is a new, independent approach. In stat-ing the objectives, management must specifically differentiate new-business development from either new-market or new-product devel-opment. If acquisitional routes are opened, the stage should be set for search and evaluation in areas of interest. If a company wants to add the sale of services to existing or future product sales or vice versa, this new direction is best described in the corporate objectives and its subsequent plan. In any case, when the capabilities of the company are underused and the basic goal is to take advantage of these com-petences and strengths, strong reference to this intent in the cor-porate objectives stimulates the forces necessary to realize it. The opportunity to use fallow talents is generally met with enthusiasm by employees.

In a multidivisional or highly departmentalized organization, its various parts can often interact effectively. The use of certain manu-facturing facilities in one division, for instance, can increase the value of a product marketed by another. To coordinate and implement such efforts generally requires intense effort and support by the highest level of management. Stating the desire to support this interaction in the corporate objectives and plan lends it special credence and strengthens the role of the party responsible for carrying it out. From this phase of corporate objectives the venture group would emerge.

Fiscal Identifications

An alternative to verbal descriptions of product and market business objectives is the financial measurement of performance and goals. This is not necessarily an independent statement, but it is substantially different in that the corporate objectives are expressed in arithmetical terms. Although it would be acceptable to assume that a verbal statement of an objective with profits, return on capital, or return on investment as a criterion is a fiscal designation, specificity is lacking. Financial terminology does not differ from other general descriptions of policy concerning such subjects as growth, contribution, obligation to the community, innovation, or leadership. In the clear numerical definition of fiscal objectives priorities can be better set, and one financial factor becomes the focal point for all others. It allows continuous monitoring of corporate progress and comparison among segments of the company. Examples of these are well known, although they are handled somewhat differently by various organizations. The intent here is only to point them out, since their importance becomes increasingly evident when analyses are made in venture studies and proposals are presented to management for approval.

Return on Investment

Measuring return on investment has gained a great deal of recognition and popularity as a mathematical tool for evaluating proposed expenditures of new capital. It can also be applied to measure continuing performance. However, utilizing a mechanism to increase ROI independently of other criteria could cause cutbacks in investment, resulting in ultimate liquidation. Therefore, ROI evaluations and objectives must be part of an overall analysis of all financial aspects in the picture. To take advantage of ROI, its limitations must be recognized.

Several mathematical models have been designed to measure return on investment. It can be handled rather simply by dividing the income, or total receipts minus cost of goods and expenses, by the total investment, including permanent (or fixed) capital and operating (or working) capital in the form of accounts receivable and inventory. Multiplying by 100 gives a percentage.

$$\text{ROI} = \frac{\text{receipts} - (\text{cost of goods} + \text{expenses})}{\text{permanent} + \text{operating capital}} \times 100$$

This formula can be refined according to the individual company. What is important is not precisely how ROI is determined but rather that it is consistent and understood by the initiator, evaluator, and decision makers. Additional factors would be depreciation as an added manufacturing expense and a tax credit; the accurate appraisal of income after tax; the discounting of receipts by the investment credit or interest; and miscellaneous items such as depletion, disposal, and amortization. All this suggests that when ROI is used to measure progress in the planning scheme for corporate objectives, it must be clearly defined for all to see and understand.

Earnings per Share

The complex yardstick or earnings per share represents an important facet of company performance from the standpoint of both executives and the investing community. Shareholders measure their return in dividends or capital appreciation. As the value or traded price of the stock increases because of the elevation of earnings per share or the anticipation of such a rise, the greater the benefit to shareholder and corporation alike. Of course, this return cannot be separated from the investment required to do the job; hence the importance of ROI and some of the succeeding quantitative measures.

Earnings per share is a generally defined number in the corporate annual report. The disadvantage of this in regard to New Venture Methodology is that it is difficult to break out the contribution of a minor business component from the corporate structure. In a new business derived independently without a corporate umbrella, these earnings become a significant figure to the potential suppliers of venture capital. One method of describing earnings per share when new stock is not used to supply the capital for the venture is to convert the dollar-investment requirements arithmetically into existing stock values and assume a corresponding offering of new issues to cover those capital needs.

Sales Factors

The quantitative analytical tools used may include several sales relationships. The corporate objective might be to achieve an increase in the percentage of profit per dollar of sales. This is measured by dividing profits by total sales and multiplying by 100. It is appropriate for certain businesses to use this where the investment is disproportionately great or small relative to sales. When investment is exceedingly low, for instance, but expense items such as labor are high, ROI will not indicate that there is a need for intensified, high-volume selling to reach a reasonable level of profit.

The ratio of sales to total assets or turnover is a measure of earn-ing efficiency. This is used in combination with the operating ratio, or expenses divided by receipts. High asset turnover with a low operating ratio is considered good performance and should produce a substantial return on the investment made. In any case, the operating margin, which is the difference between receipts and the costs of producing goods for sale, should be sufficiently large to support the sales and administration expenses and still deliver profits.

Growth curves depicting sales with time and profits with time are other indicators that can be used for quantification of corporate objectives. Other sales-directed factors and ratios can be developed to describe corporate expansion. These are useful tools for management, provided that the objectives define the appropriate use of the method and its terms.

In summary, we include a reminder that net worth, present value, discounted cash flow, and other quantitative relationships dealing with the financial aspects of business can be used. The reason for delving into these areas in regard to New Venture Methodology is to inform all those involved in venture efforts of the broad possibilities of the approaches. The planning that occurs at the primary level of management, whether in a large corporate entity, a segment of it, a small business, or an entrepreneur's effort within or outside these entities, is the foundation for planning new ventures.

Venture Planning

A venture is an implemented plan. When a specific plan for a venture is described, it becomes immediately apparent that the whole of this text prepares for moving into a growth-oriented, viable, profitable new business, which in turn influences corporate dynamics. Thus the venture plan is a scheme for formally devising an appropriate program. The means of mounting the venture is the entire New Venture Methodology. This statement, however, is too broad and gives little guidance for concisely channeling the type of plans imperative for venture accomplishment.

The venture plans supplement management projections from destiny planning to corporate objectives. The first stage is a description of the scope of the corporation, its resources, capabilities, talents, manpower, knowledge, and activities. Once such a document is complete, it can be used as the basis for successive ventures, provided that a continuous effort is made to keep it current. There are several ways to prepare the venture plan background. Whereas the small businessman can do this job with a minimum of time and effort, the larger, more diverse corporation cannot. Even for the small company or independent businessman, to execute this task is revealing and educational, and when done pragmatically and unemotionally it will clearly demonstrate the needs and complications when a venture is being seriously considered. A relatively complex chart (Figure 1) demonstrates one technique. It can be simplified or expanded to fit the circumstances of the organization. As the boxes are filled in, the aspects of the company that lend themselves to expansion, the fields and disciplines where strengths and weaknesses exist, and the basic opportunities that are ripe or potential are revealed.

Whatever the developed chart looks like, in a specific case it should be designed to give an overall description of current operations and capacities. This general information, coupled with the corporate plans, allows development of a basic strategy and expected results from the venture during a fixed planning period. Future goals can be specified with management's blessings, and the initial stages of New Venture Methodology can be entered. If possible, the products of the company can be quantified, with emphasis on opportunity, potential, profit, market, flexibility, and creativity.

The venture planning presented in the following discussion is divided into three basic aspects, all related to the overall methodology. The first is a definition of the steps in a venture. The second is a measure of the venture and its success. The third is a description of scheduling that relates to the time and cost elements of the venture plan.

Venture Sequence

The sequence most representative of a new venture comprises five stages: (1) inception, (2) analysis, (3) development, (4) commercialization, and (5) growth. Each of these leads directly to the next. The first, inception, entails several measures, including a general strategic plan, a search for a workable opportunity, the selection of an optimum route and operation, and the organization necessary for putting the primary plan to work.

The next step is the complex task of analysis, in which specific business activities and various quantitative and detailed evaluations begin. A need analysis would be made to insure that the choice is indeed a proper one. In the case of a technological advance, a market must be found, and the justification for moving into a totally new and often undefinable area should be demonstrated in the need analysis. Of course, a market study using simulation models would follow.

Figure 1. Scope of corporate resources.

| | Divisions | | | | | Corporate |
| | A | | | B | C | Total |
	Product I	Product II	Product III			
Raw materials						
Basic						
Processed						
Intermediate						
Finished						
Unit products						
Components						
Assemblies						
Devices						
Structures						
Marketing						
Research						
Direct sales						
Indirect sales						
Advertising						
Warehousing						
Distributing						
Contacts						
Technical						
Disciplines						
Research						
Services						
Testing						
Consultants						
Planning						
Management						
Services						
Priorities						
Administration						
Resources						
Manufacturing						
Engineering						
Processes						
Evaluation						
Cost estimating						
Financial						
Funding						
Timing						
Growth						

In the market analysis, a subsection covering sales, distribution, and pricing would be included. With a product whose technology is not new, a study of the technology to be used would be required for solving any potential problems, including patent status. The use of engineering and manufacturing analyses is important where a production technique new to the company is involved or where facilities would be modified to fill production needs. The financial analysis is among the most important to corporate management or the supplier of venture capital. Since the ultimate goal is profitability, this analysis is given priority by the funding source. As we shall discuss further on, financial analysis becomes an integral and major portion of the venture proposal. Legal analysis may be made where there are questions involving contracts, purchases, or joint agreements. In any case, an opinion on the relevant legal matters is better made before proceeding to the action phase than after expenditures for business entry are made.

The following list shows other analyses or considerations, including a segment called "venture analysis." This term is used here because it has a specific meaning in the discipline of new-business evaluation. It represents a somewhat narrower analysis than the combined structured ones outlined in this list.

Need analysis	Patent situation
Market analysis	Miscellaneous
Sales	Acquisitions
Distribution	Testing and test marketing
Pricing	Operations
Technical analysis	Venture analysis
Engineering analysis	Mathematical models
Manufacturing analysis	Flow diagrams
Financial analysis	Risk and sensitivity
Legal analysis	Comparative charting

These analyses summarize the growth potential in the endeavor, rating research contribution and effort, market needs and potentials, production capacity and capability, and changes in the business climate. The concepts and questions included at this stage of planning are those that lead to evaluation of the chance for business success and the viability of the market as these relate to dollar burden and investment.

The third phase, called venture development, is actually market development. It includes performance testing, field testing, opinion panels, visits to customers, and test marketing. This is the prelude to commercialization, which follows the successful completion of stage 3. As the venture matures, the anticipation of growth into a profitable business, meeting the projections in sales and returns, is the principle on which everything is predicated.

To demonstrate how dollars are spent during this five-step venture sequence, Figure 2 shows a curve of cash flow on a relative scale. It indicates that the most money is spent during commercialization when a major part of the investment is allocated. The rewards are reaped when the line operation begins its payback during the commercialization stage and continuing into the mature business phase.

Venture Measurement

The importance of venture measurement as a part of planning cannot be overstated. The development of a direct, concise, and meaningful rating system early in the venture is critical to planning and monitoring. Discussion of measuring the contribution of ventures to corporate growth and profits occurs in later chapters. The major consideration at this point should be the choice of an appropriate plan for candid evaluation and numerical and fiscal rating. Several general approaches are available that serve in much the same way as the expression of corporate objectives: to direct the selection of the venture, to clarify the proposal, to describe its contribution, and to effect control.

Sales performance. When a plot of forecast sales is drawn using a logarithmic scale and a five-year period on the two axes, many ques-

Figure 2. Cash flow with time, showing venture sequence steps.

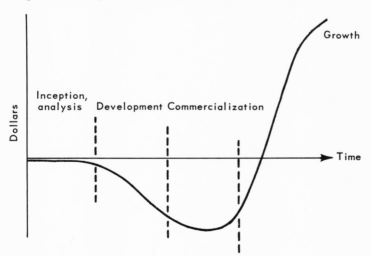

tions can be answered. The five-year period is not sacrosanct, and it may be preferable to use a ten-year term, provided one recognizes the lower reliability of the later projections. In all cases, the desired result is a straight line. When the line begins to curve downward, the rate of growth is diminishing though growth itself continues. The actual sales performance should be compared with the forecast dollar volume. This may be a different figure from the early projections, because as business climates change and experience is gained, new forecasts will be made that deviate from the original expectation.

Profit description. Like sales performance, profits can be plotted. It must first be determined whether the profit is an overall gain, before or after taxes, taking into account other factors that affect the profit figure, or a contribution to the general corporate profit when a parent organization is involved. This is a good tool to use in conjunction with the sales curve, since it shows the meaning of sales growth in terms of profit goals even during periods of loss.

Cash flow. Another measure of the venture is the cash flow over a given period. It relates sales and profit information to investment and other financial factors. Cash for investment is included in ROI studies, but deficit or budget spending in early venture operations does not affect the investment figure; hence it is not obvious in the year-to-year ROI figures. These costs are an inherent part of cash flow. On a chart or graph showing cash flow, which is the cumulative difference between expenditures and profit on an incremental time-period basis, the point at which investment is returned through receipts is the payback. Cash flow also describes the break-even point. This is the minimum in the curve, since the business no longer requires new funds.

Payout. Payout occurs on the cash-flow graph where cumulative dollar deficits in investment, fixed and operating, along with day-to-day expenditures for running the business, are equal to generated cash. Again, the specific definition of terms to be used for evaluating the business must be included in the plan. Obviously, variations in what is classified as expenditure, investments, income, and profit can significantly alter the shape of the curves we discussed and change the time element materially. All these proposed financial tools can be used effectively for judging the progress and performance of a new venture.

Scheduling

Time is an important element in any plan. Specific dates for completing tasks are set in such planning devices as CPM, PERT, and

Figure 3. Planning and scheduling chart.

Period	Months																								
	Weeks																								
Objectives																									
Product description																									
Product specifications																									
Performance needs																									
Value in use																									
Process description																									
Initial production																									
Commerical manufacture																									
Market description																									
Distribution																									
Pricing																									
Sales strategy																									
Financial analysis																									
Cost of producing																									
Investment																									
Manpower costs																									
Field test expenses																									
Production costs																									
Sales expenses																									

Gantt charts. While these are helpful tools and allow the scheduling of pertinent decision points, there are some simple alternatives. No doubt the use of many sophisticated techniques is recommended under proper circumstances, but initial planning can be satisfactorily carried out using a chart or table such as that in Figure 3. Here the task can be described in a general sense without itemizing in detail all the steps required to achieve it. The various jobs or categories are listed in the order that they should be accomplished: an order of priority, an order of cost, or a sequence of time periods required to complete them. A calendar plot by month or by week can be used to show the beginning and end of the project phase and the period required to accomplish it. Adding a summation of costs and an estimation of manpower needs allows rapid, in-depth determination of the demands of the program on the organization.

Another way to schedule the venture would be to plan it according to its analysis. Referring to Figure 3, one can give the various analytic segments an order similar to the functional tasks required for the development of the project shown in Figure 3. In addition, a study of previous products from inception to commercialization can provide reference points. Project phases can be listed according to the objectives rather than the task. For example, instead of field testing, which is the task, the objectives of the field test such as customer acceptance, color preference, or some other property or characteristic would be scheduled for completion on specific dates.

In the course of planning, many operations are performed. In New Venture Methodology, some definite approach to planning must be used. Flexibility and recognition of the potential benefits should direct the type and degree of planning executed by the venture leader. Since new ventures are implemented plans or at the very least revolve about a central corporate program, planning is a first-order consideration.

3

The Organization

A<small>N</small> essential part of preparing for a successful venture program is the serious consideration that must be given the organization of the venture group. Its essence, objectives, structure, flow, interrelationships, support, and people must be in concord with the structure of the company to insure effective use of New Venture Methodology. A company or an individual must locate a particular approach that best meets its need in light of its own situation. Much attention has been given to the proper positioning of the new-product department, which will be discussed partly for comparative purposes. Although its position is important to operate effectively, the most critical aspect is not its place in the hierarchical structure but commitment to a new-venture effort rather than new-product development by the company's highest-level decision makers. Once such a commitment is stated that new opportunities will be explored and exploited for growth purposes, organizational matters become an important if not critical step for successful action and participation in venturing.

Staffing

Before New Venture Methodology can be put into operation, the people who will use it must be considered. Whether one is dealing with companies whose strengths are in technical, merchandising, manufacturing, or marketing disciplines, the most important part of a new venture program is its leadership. Men who can pull together the many data areas and meld the various aggressive venture personalities into a unified effort are invaluable. The nucleus of a new-product group must consist of gifted entrepreneurs, supported by people with the desire, intent, and devotion to make a success of their venture. Not all gifted people are entrepreneurs, and business acumen is learned, not inherited. Creativity and education alone are not necessarily the mark of the entrepreneur.

Entrepreneurs

Historically, successful new-product developments have been attributed to people whose creative talents, singleness of purpose, and self-motivation have supplied the business and technical impetus. They are the entrepreneurs. It is with enlightened hindsight that such people are recognized. But if a development fails, would an adventurer be any less an entrepreneur? Conversely, are all successful managers—those fortunate enough to have a good product— necessarily entrepreneurs? The critical point is that entrepreneurs are recognized after the fact, once a market success is acknowledged and not before. The nascent leader must therefore be described in terms other than those of past achievements, for so many potential managers are denied the opportunity that would enable them to earn the title *entrepreneur*. Some of the factors involved in describing, locating, stimulating, and rewarding the talented, well-equipped person are best revealed indirectly through an analysis of the organization of the new group that is to carry out the new-business task, for he must integrate and coordinate its operations.

Source of leaders. Venture leaders are found in many obvious positions throughout the corporation, through outside sources, and in various other ways. In small companies or in one-man operations, the leader is usually the inventor, founder, or president. The most fruitful areas to search are among product-oriented technical specialists and technically oriented marketing people. This suggestion has implications far beyond the simplicity of its words. The search should not be inflexible; it should not necessarily be limited to people with these backgrounds. A talented, aggressive man with a creative bent can be found in any activity or discipline, within the company or outside it. When searching internally, the large company has a distinct advantage. Corporate staff groups supply fertile ground for training and evaluating candidates for venture work. While the tendency is to look among product innovators as a primary source, line functions can also provide highly motivated people who are well equipped for venture leadership. It would be impertinent for a lay writer to delve into the psychology of a leader, in ventures or out of them, but it would also be negligent to omit a brief description of the groundwork for selecting one.

Characteristics of the entrepreneur. The key man and his lieutenants, if one assumes that the operation is to be of some consequence, should be experienced in various functions. While new-product development is highly desirable, research experience might reasonably substitute for it. Exposure to manufacturing, marketing, and line sales provides a broad understanding of the many components required for a new business to be successfully inaugurated. For candidates from outside the company, previous new-product experience in a unidirectional group is most desirable. Age is a consideration, and although a boundary cannot be precisely set upon it, maturity at a young age or a seasoned man with a youthful temperament (a statement deliberately vague) is the goal.

Personal characteristics, in the final analysis, are the best criteria. A man well trained and educated in several fields and business disciplines who is enthusiastic, energetic but not overbearing, dedicated, self-starting, communicative, decisive, gregarious, conversant with modern techniques, and consistent yet flexible and who shows a sense of urgency in all his activities should make the type of leader required. This idealized description fits almost no one, yet most good men have a portion of all these characteristics. The object is to find a balance of these characteristics, in one person, all designed to fit the particular position. He should be capable of planning, budgeting, scheduling, and coordinating product operations. He serves as liaison with various staff members and trains venture analysts to function within the group. He must vigorously pursue developments and help to achieve a proprietary position for the company. He must develop areas of potential profitability, expand and diversify the corporate position, and enhance the corporate growth. He is easily recognized by his desire to succeed and his generally apparent need to perform and to succeed.

Personnel

In order to avoid many levels of organization, the remaining group members will be picked to supplement the fine leaders previously chosen. These people will not necessarily be generalists; each should be especially strong in one discipline. This is not to say they are limited specialists, since they will need to function in many areas and hopefully will generate the support required for a continual flow of new ventures. They are the good performers from campuses, departments, manufacturing plants, and the field. They have strong personalities and are self-motivated and prepared to work within a loose organizational structure. These people must be ready to accept rapid change, various challenges, quick decisions. They must show early maturity and should themselves be incipient leaders. The most desirable qualities among the venture staff are diversity of experience, both disciplinary and functional, with an especially strong desire and commitment to make a particular venture succeed.

Size

The major benefit of instituting New Venture Methodology is that the size of a venture group and subsequently the expense can be effectively controlled; it can and should remain as small as possible within the confines of efficient performance. When one person has all the responsibility, as in a small company or one-man venture operation or in the initial development of a venture group in any corporation, there is little structure to discuss. When an opportunity is recognized, studied, and presented, however, that person should be designated to pursue it. Continuation of the new-venture approach is in jeopardy unless a replacement is readily at hand. For this reason, the leader should be supplemented by another person very early in the selection phase of a new opportunity, preferably before any firm commitment is made to a business development. The alternate can then serve as prime mover or as the new functioning leader of venture search when the original one is designated entrepreneur and manager of the new business. If a small, intense group is used to analyze the opportunity in depth, then its members should be assigned full time to the program, not on a part-time basis with shared time and job responsibility. This group is and remains a separate unit independent of other operational or staff ties.

Organization

Organizing the department or group to carry out the functions that nurture a program from inception to commercialization is integral to New Venture Methodology. Organization problems are well recognized, and studies have reported that 80 percent of the companies involved in new-product activity cite them as a primary concern. There is not a single or simple standard for the proper organization structure, size, or shape that serves the development of new business. There are, however, specific basic concepts that thread through various organizational approaches and that have been tailored to individual company needs.

The venture organization should be separate from other operational functions. When it remains independent with a singleness of purpose, it lowers risk and saves time and money. The structure of the venture organization does not follow any universal rules, but certain general criteria for optimum operation should be adhered to for best results. Some of these points may seem obvious, but they are too often violated.

Let us start with a basic organization in which all personnel report to the leader of the group. This implies no middle management. A scheme showing three representative new-venture operations is seen in Figure 4. The first (A) is a small team that can be easily structured to meet the needs of the individual company. There is nothing sacrosanct about the labels used here, but it is necessary to have people available with capabilities in market research and marketing and in product and process and with overall financial competence. Any of these three analysts will be in a position to lead a subgroup if a viable venture opportunity within his capacities is discovered.

The second organization in Figure 4 (B) can be viewed as a more mature operation or a venture approach by a larger, more dedicated, or more generously budgeted corporate body. This group can supply all its own needs, including limited prototypes and product definition and demonstration. The various portions of the feasibility study, the venture description, and analysis become a direct function of the group.

In the third diagram (C), the ventures segment remains the same in structure but supplemental organizations are tied to it through common management. A product-development (or process development) group performs an adjacent function with much broader capabilities and responsibilities than the venture team would have in this activity. The product-development operation would supply additional talents, physically describe new products or processes, and meet specifications for products set by the operating divisions or by a particular venture team. The product-development group may also supply whatever product is needed to run test marketing, field demonstrations, or other confirmatory work. Those product development people working on a venture project might eventually become part of the venture team. Commercial development is a much-needed part of the scheme in that it is not functional or appropriate to put a mature venture synonymous with a commercial development operation under the same management as young, incipient ventures. The cadre for the new business is added, an operating budget is assigned, and initial sales

Figure 4. General venture organizations.

(A)

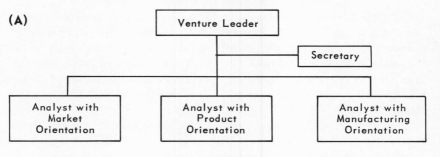

(B)

Staffed as above   **Potential team leaders**

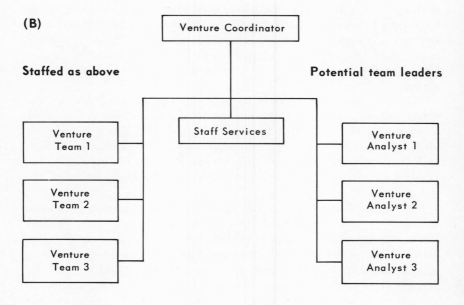

(C)

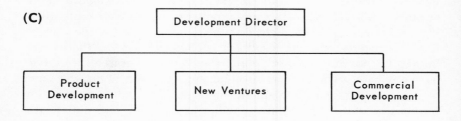

are attempted. The venture should at this point be self-contained, with diverse capabilities, and should be removed from the venture search group in order to avoid any dilution of the original effort.

To use remaining members of the venture staff in indirect support of the new business, which can occur if the move is not made early, has two detrimental effects. First, the venture search, screening, and selection function is minimized both in fact and in the minds and activities of the group. Second, among interim or temporary people the sense of belonging is not intense enough for them to recognize the critical value of their individual contributions to the venture. The use of other assistants not integral to the team for formative business or risk groups is to be avoided for similar reasons. This is not to suggest eliminating the aggressive and extensive use of specialists to assist in areas of need. In larger corporations, a task can be assigned to service groups if management accepts a high enough priority for it. Personnel generally should be assigned and budgeted for if they are actually needed. By pursuing this course, one exercises better control over money and time as they apply to people in the venture. It also allows more direct monitoring of costs in effort and dollars without specious conclusions or improperly low figures. Where it is practical, a physical move as well as an organizational one produces the best situation. Separating the venture group from its original site within the building of the parent organization gives it a sense of independence that underscores the unidirectionality of its objective.

Administration

The final accountability for new ventures lies with the chief operating officer, who should therefore have as close contact with the venture operation as is reasonable. But for day-to-day administration, the high-level administrator is either a corporate R&D vice-president or the corporate development vice-president. People involved even at higher management levels, however, should and will change as the character of the venture changes. Initially, a minimum of organizational levels should be placed between the leader or entrepreneur and the financial decision maker, and none is preferable. This suggests that the top venture man should answer to the chief operating officer.

Figures 5, 6, 7, and 8 show how best to design the new venture organization. These charts depict effective structures at different stages in the development of a business opportunity. In Figure 5, a small group of incipient entrepreneurs coordinate and guide an exploration for new business opportunities. This is a search, screening, and select-

ing group that performs a budgeted staff function. It should not be regarded or used as a market research group, a market review board, or
a product-testing team. Its members can give part-time assistance to
development functions within the company. Holding this to a minimum is difficult once the venture group's efficiency and capacity for
response are recognized. Repeated incursions into its work and areas
of interest can be disturbing and eventually demoralizing. The search
group functions as an interdivisional liaison to keep the venture
group informed and to be kept informed.

The exploration group operates under an independent code of action, and its one goal is to find, individually rather than collectively,
business opportunities at such a state of development that a company
can capitalize on them. When such a discovery is made (though perhaps it is more an uncovering than a discovery), certain justifying
documents must be prepared. These will be discussed later. The corporate decision to proceed has more to do with faith and confidence
by management in the person who has identified the opportunity than

Figure 5. A new-venture organization.

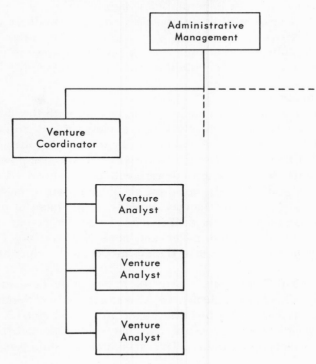

Figure 6. Formation of venture teams.

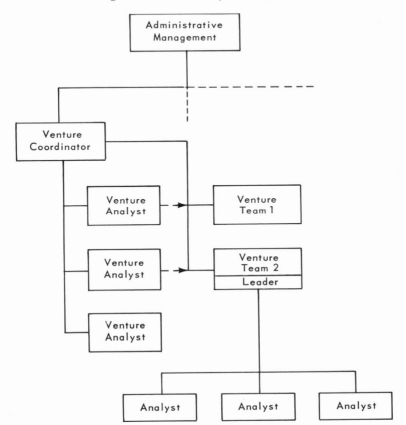

in the paper and reports he produces. At this point, it is too early to be sure how extensive the opportunity will be. To help determine that, the program enters a phase of intense analysis and evaluation, for which a venture team is formed. Its leader will be one of the entrepreneurs or analysts, as shown in Figure 5, but not necessarily the coordinator, who might have to function as permanent administrator for the teams when the number of teams and groups becomes too unwieldy for those at the next-higher management level to handle comfortably.

Figure 6 shows two or three members added to the venture team, chosen according to the needs of the project. Very few people are needed to reach a decision about the viability of the new concept or business opportunity. At this time, an evaluative tool, such as a venture-worth forecast or modified decision-analysis study form, should be developed on the basis of the projected value of the venture and its chances for technical and commercial success. This tool would be formulated to produce a numerical rating that could be used as part of the planning phase for comparative purposes. The newly appointed leader would determine the composition and the proper time to set up a team. The selection would then probably indicate the need for further detailed study. It is highly improbable that a thorough job would be done without several participants, because a variety of in-depth talents are required for a good venture analysis and business proposal. The task is not so simple that one person, no matter how talented, could handle it in a short time. Further, the flow of ideas from new people on the team can shed new light on the direction or efficiency of the program and help eliminate uncertainty in areas of factual weakness. Administrative management is kept fully informed during this time, usually through oral presentation. The funds should remain part of the developmental budget; there is no need for separate appropriations. If seed funds are not planned for when the venture method is started, this approach is in jeopardy from the beginning.

The next step is a critical one. The team has prepared a detailed report on the opportunity and is ready to proceed. The work has been generally internal, with perhaps little tangible evidence of product or process. A prototype should be in hand to support a product description, although it is not required if the features of the product are obvious. A major increase in size of the venture team's operation is planned at this point, and a substantial increase in spending is contemplated. The presentation of the proposal and the request for funds should be made to an executive control committee authorized to allow the expenditure. The basis for the authorization of funds should not be a sales forecast but a general market-potential and time-penetration curve.

This authorization permits the establishment of risk groups, such as those shown in Figure 7. The risk group provides a basis for taking the opportunity to the marketplace. The projected expenses for the life of the group, until it is successful or dissolved, should be openly stated. A profit-and-loss statement has little meaning at this time, although when sales are made, many companies require one. Anticipated sales account for part of the operating budget of the risk group; in this elemental business form, however, the operation should not be viewed as income producing but as total expense. The problem with justifying a risk group by using a pro forma profit-and-loss statement is that the project is sufficiently prognostic in character to make the value or meaning of P&L minimal. It is also possible that within a short time the decision to proceed will be reversed, since the risk group is still only testing the market, the product, and the internal capabilities to produce economically.

With no formal fiscal control as we propose here, it is incumbent upon administrative management (the next-higher level of executive responsibility, such as vice-president of development) to take first-line management responsibility. This is coincidental with the removal of the risk group from the coordinator. As separate operations, both the venture group and the risk group benefit from maintaining integrity and unidirectionality. The risk group moves beyond the analytic function of the venture team to test marketing. Tools such as an oper-

Figure 7. Formation of risk groups.

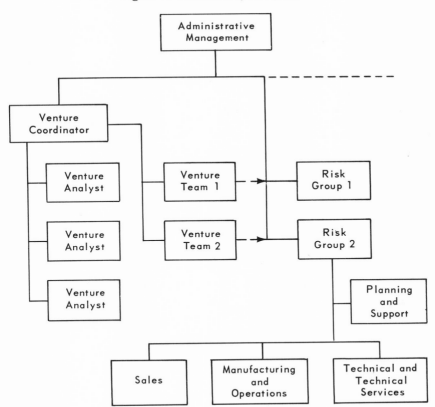

ational planning document and constant monitoring of a venture-worth number are needed in this stage of development.

Figure 8 shows the next two stages combined. Assuming success by the risk group in meeting predetermined objectives and demonstrating the vitality of an opportunity and a high probability of commercial success, we would propose a development plan. This is an important procedure because major expenditures are required. Chapters 7, 9, and 10 discuss in depth the proposal, commercial development, and maturation. The important organizational developments to note are the changes in structure of the operation, realignment of tasks and responsibilities, and management control.

In a venture of any reasonable magnitude, sales and manufacturing will be among the key functions, as they are in any operating business. Service activities will be proportionately higher, however, to insure a strong entry into the marketplace in the initial phases. At this point, the entrepreneur becomes a line manager and must adopt the techniques of a profit-oriented business. A formal P&L account is instituted and sales and profits accurately forecast on the basis of the experience of up to two years as a risk group. P&L will then be con-

Figure 8. Venture commercialization.

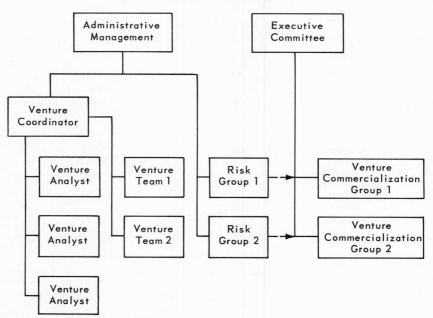

tinuously monitored. The remaining members of the original venture team will be placed in operational positions that require quite different talents from those called for on the original team. The excitement of introducing a new business to the company and to the industrial or consumer community becomes the satisfaction of keeping a machine well oiled, tuned, and moving. The venture commercialization group no longer reports to the same administrative management as the risk groups but is directly responsible to a small, select committee of top-line executives. (There is no justification for a commercial operation to be housed under a staff unit.) One of these executives is key adviser to and monitor for the general manager of the commercialization group. It is not inconceivable that this adviser is vice-president of development. Or he could be a divisional vice-president whose division is heir apparent to the commercial development. Finally, at maturation of the opportunity, a new line organization is started or an operating division inherits the business as part of its function.

Alternative Organization Approaches

No discussion of organization would be complete without several specific examples of how new-product development and new ventures are handled by a number of corporations. Emphasis will be on those most closely related to New Venture Methodology and less like the new-product-development groups frequently described by other authors. For comparison, some of the approaches presented are quite far removed from the most highly recommended organizational structure. Alternative approaches are of several types, as distinguished by the venture group's management, the function within which it is located, and operational methods.

Product or brand managers. Two management approaches to new business are well known and used by numerous companies. They employ the product-manager and brand-manager structures. They are marketing-oriented and usually are located within the marketing segment of the company. They differ in scope and market orientation but are basically the same in that new products compete with existing lines for time, effort, and funds. New products being developed tend to be classified with those currently handled, and usually no new staffs or distribution methods are required. These approaches have proved successful as ways to implement product-line extensions or product improvements.

Product development. Organizational approaches of this kind can be divided into three major classifications:

1. A new-product department within a divisional structure that responds to the general manager. It is usually limited to the product line of the division and basically concerns products rather than needs or opportunities.
2. A new-product group within the technical or engineering function. It supports the introduction of ideas, inventions, and innovations developed internally. The weakest parts of this approach are that it is often given improper market guidance and there is a tendency to oversupport research developments with questionable business futures.
3. A new-product department within the marketing function. Here the need is magnified, response to customer curiosity is often overemphasized, and recognition of the development time, manufacturing costs, and investment is minimal.

Each of these alternatives lacks the integration of thought, goals, objectives, and functions that is critical to successful new-product development.

Other general approaches. A brief survey of other approaches that have been attempted, suggested, or are still in use reveals a constant search for a mechanism to do the job consistently and under various circumstances. Each has advantages, but most lack the coordination, cross-fertilization, unidirectionality, and commitment that New Venture Methodology offers.

1. Task force. This has been a successful approach when specific objectives have been defined. It is responsive but tends to create a crisis atmosphere. It is temporary in nature, and any follow-through beyond the initial limited objective is infrequent.
2. Committee. Much has been said about this controversial approach. It has the power to advise but seldom to act. It transfers responsibility, coordinates efforts, and relies upon acceptance and action by many nonmembers.
3. Think group. This is the antithesis of the task force. Whereas the latter is action-oriented toward an objective, the think group is free to roam about many objectives. This activity tends to offer alternatives rather than solutions and usually leaves implementation to others.
4. Support team. Here is another temporary function used to give a helping hand to the responsible and accountable agency. The commitment is limited, training time is often excessive, and goals are predefined and act as boundaries on the support team. There is an implied make-it-work-no-matter-what attitude attached to this technique.

Organization Structures

Chemical company. Figure 9 shows the structure of a newly formed group as announced by a medium-size chemical company. The basic structure is a variation of the third type shown in Figure 4 (C). The product-development function is organizationally adjacent to the new-venture groups and has common management. The enterprise manager's additional responsibility as divisional liaison should have little effect on the operation of the group. The major deficiency here is that there is no apparent opportunity-defining group outside of product development. The venture teams are functionally involved in a venture with the implication that the new leaders are involved in product development. To be more effective, a separate function, perhaps within the product-development group (though it should be distinct and not limited by the group's activities), could be established to recognize, analyze, and mobilize the best possible opportunities for venture team status. It would also be appropriate to have mature teams, such as our risk groups, eventually report directly to the vice-president of development (see Figure 9). One reason for establishing a venture group is actually to handle product developments not being exploited by the parent organization. This is a pragmatic task, sometimes resulting in less than a fully operative venture approach. The group should be committed to the development of ventures, and not just remain content to inherit idle potential opportunities or technical curiosities.

Industrial products company. In Figure 10, another rather typical approach is outlined. This industrial products company is a large operation that developed this method over several years. As the figure

Figure 9. Medium-size chemical company venture organization.

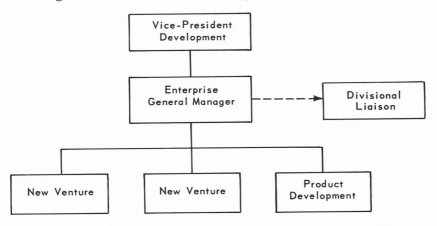

shows, the venture division vice-president is much more than the entrepreneur. He is a major administrative leader in the corporation. The use of service functions to support research and to initiate a team is antipathetic to the methods of New Venture Methodology. The basic disparities lie in

- The use of staff services rather than their incorporation into the venture analysts' group or the venture team.
- The lack of transition from research to a commercial development group.
- The commercial development group's reporting to the same management as research and market segments.

When service groups are the sources of study and opportunity generation, the risk of duplication and limited analysis within each sphere of expertise is heightened. There is no central driving force to bring along new business opportunities. Such an organization is formed by evolution, whereas the intended function of the venture division is to assist in other people's ventures. When it doesn't work, it is combined with the venture groups to give common management a chance to force the issue. But it will still suffer, for New Venture Methodology would require all functions necessary for successful venturing to be within the venture itself. Further, the analysts directly responsible for initiating ventures should not be service-oriented but entrepreneurially directed. The transition from laboratory to commercial development could then proceed systematically.

Figure 10. Industrial products company venture organization.

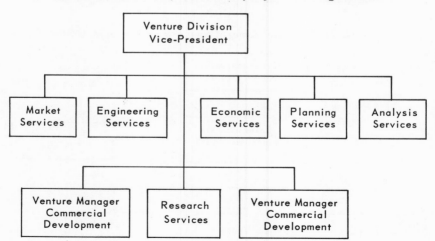

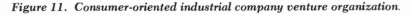

Figure 11. Consumer-oriented industrial company venture organization.

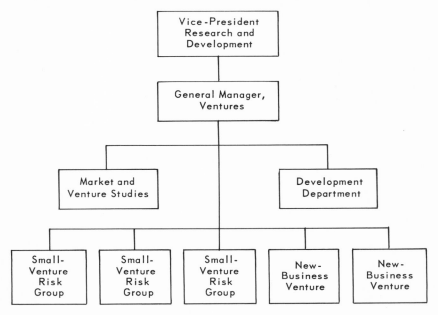

Consumer-oriented industrial company. This organization is much more complex, and similar schemes have been discussed by various authors. Figure 11 contains most of the characteristics of New Venture Methodology as applied in a consumer-oriented business. Its size and maturity have led to certain variations that have been successful for this company. These variations are readily handled within the contexts of their specific objectives without violating basic principles. The technical and marketing functions work together in a coordinated effort to provide the product as well as information and guidance for the nascent ventures, while determining the market need. This scheme has guarded against the association of the venture development and small businesses with an operating corporate arm. It avoids the pitfall of sharing venture development time, money, and effort with the new business that is concentrating on the production, distribution, sales, and product improvement so critical to supporting a healthy and profitable business. Short-term programs emerging from a support role usually create an environment that diminishes the flexibility needed to explore unique business areas. To maintain a long-range approach free from potential restrictions or from encroachment during periods of immediate problem solving, permitting the group independence is a necessary management commitment.

The physical proximity of the development people and those examining the business climate is another important aspect of this approach. The benefit of organizing a special group to create new businesses within the corporate entity is that it is designed to accomplish that task. The only flaw is that the new-business venture groups do not become independent soon enough. It would be preferable to have them report directly to the vice-president of research and development or his counterpart elsewhere in the company. It is interesting to note that the development department reports to the general manager of ventures, giving him a built-in source of new-product or new-process opportunities.

Diverse product and service company. As indicated in Figure 12, the business development organization in this diverse service- and product-oriented corporation carries the administrative burden of the venture groups, but is basically a staff organization. There are no defined mechanisms for search, screening, and selecting within this loosely structured operation. High-caliber people of diverse interests and talents can produce a plethora of potential business opportunities through a common management. The number of marginal ventures that could be derived from this method indicates the need for a better organizational approach. Aside from those who control the choice of a venture, using people who are not assigned to the venture weakens the approach. One cannot, however, fault the use of a general management advisory board or the venture manager's exercising direct capability in many disciplines within his purview. He can use men from his specialists' groups to carry out the search, give guidance to research people (hence the dotted line from the research division to specialists), and develop multidisciplinary talents. The load on the vice president of development restricted his ability to take advantage of internally developed opportunities. The formation of a new-venture approach was an outgrowth of this, and originated from the loosely organized staff of advisory people who had originally served as the vice-president's council. Again, the partial commitment to attempt to handle an obvious shortcoming led to a complicated and not-too-successful organization.

Equipment and materials company. The organization described in Figure 13 represents a technique for staffing after a venture has been initiated in the equipment and materials field. There is apparently no recognized need for the new-venture department to explore and find those opportunities most appropriate for the company. The unfortunate part of making such a facile assumption is that opportunities or venture candidates seldom appear or develop spontaneously or in so mature a form as that resulting from efforts through the New Venture Methodology scheme. This type of approach presupposes, or at least relies upon, other corporate areas to supply its ventures. It has some distinct virtues as a commercial development organ, but lacks the vitality needed to be an originator of business opportunities.

Manufacturing-oriented company. Figure 14 illustrates a new-product-development approach in a manufacturing-oriented company. The intent, attention, and support are supplied, but the design is such that only limited, internally generated ventures can be expected, bringing with them some of the significant problems of pres-

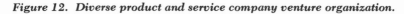

Figure 12. Diverse product and service company venture organization.

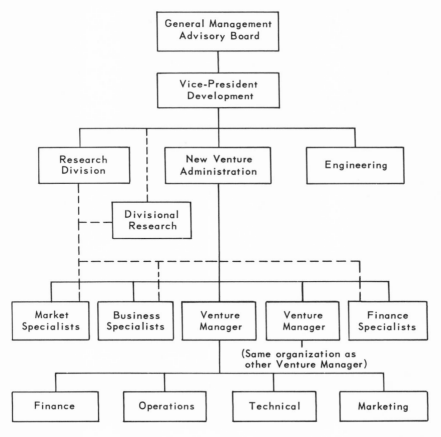

ent product-development techniques. In this case, the spawning ground for the next group of entrepreneurs is not readily apparent. It also presents the complex problem of melding research, product development, and commercial development under one managerial head, all competing for support through money and manpower. In an organization of this size, separation of the venture group is recommended.

Here is a classical approach to commodity products through new-product-development techniques. All functions are present without the coordinated organization and effort required for rapid action. The processes of analysis, development, and planning are duplicated. No dynamic, unidirectional unit exists for proper exploitation. It is overburdened with nonfunctional groups. The commercial development function is present, but the businesses are housed outside its responsibility. A thorough look at this organization, which has produced several new products but no truly new and profitable businesses, is required to make it more amenable to New Venture Methodology.

Small specialty instruments company. In the preceding cases we were concerned with organizations with large dollar volumes in sales. It is obvious that the types of structural entities developed to bring about their growth, and hopefully profits, in business are also large,

Figure 13. Equipment and materials company venture organization.

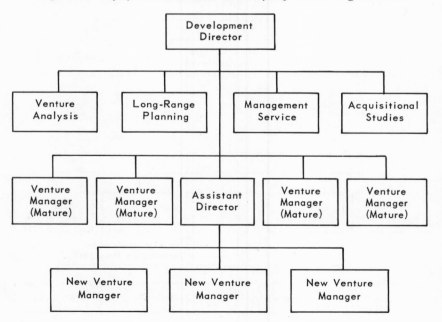

Figure 14. New-product development organization.

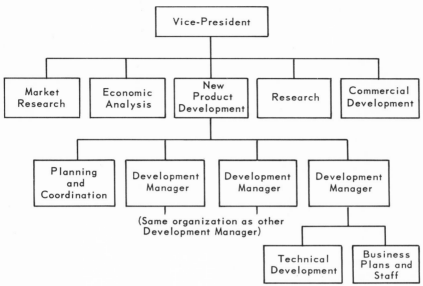

quite varied, and sometimes unwieldy. When a small, specialty instruments company, such as that indicated in Figure 15, is examined,
its simplicity becomes apparent. The chief operating officer integrates
all the day-to-day activities of the company, but has limited resources
to promote new products and new ventures. His advantage is that he
probably was, only a short time ago, the entrepreneur who has now

Figure 15. Small specialty instruments company venture organization.

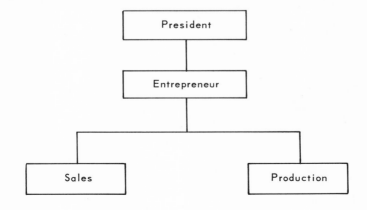

succeeded. He may still play that role, but he is usually ineffective at it owing to the press of other duties. It may be better for him to turn over the operating function to someone else while he returns to his primary talent. Either way, only a talented, thoroughly committed, and strongly motivated man will survive as entrepreneur in this highly visible position. The two or three more people involved in the venture must make it work quickly, inexpensively, and with little assistance. Although other components of New Venture Methodology are used, little is left to the imagination concerning the proper type of venture method or organization plan to use; it is obvious.

Small industrial specialty products company. In Figure 16, a smaller, industrial-specialty-products company's venture organization is outlined. All technical output, new business, and expansion of the product line emanates from the vice-president of development. One man serves as chief long-range planner, market researcher, and opportunity searcher. He is supported by an analyst, who has characterized the opportunity, determined its soundness, and described its needs in terms of new input and a general plan for implementation. The venture manager is responsible for developing, manufacturing, and marketing.

As soon as a satisfactory business is identified, the innovation moves into the corporate line organization. The venture manager is ready for the next one. In this case a flow of people does not occur. The number of people and the time in which to demonstrate the possibilities are limited. Change occurs rapidly, and the reliability of the

*Figure 16. Small industrial specialty products company
venture organization.*

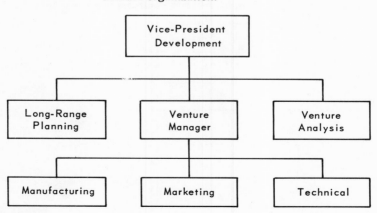

process is measured by the success of the promoted ventures. This is a lean approach that can and does work. Because venturing with New Venture Methodology is designed to afford the advantages of a small company in its rapidity of action and decision making, the virtues of the organization indicated here are apparent. The approach in this small, profitable, and growing concern was developed through trial and error, and was found to work best in its present structure. It is an example of the multidisciplined and unidirectional nature that New Venture Methodology so strongly advocates.

Organization is important to successful use of New Venture Methodology. It must be tailored to the objectives of the company. The right one does not in itself insure any degree of success, but it certainly allows a more orderly and easily monitored venture flow. Without proper attention to a well-defined, planned organization, complications in operation can overshadow desired productivity. A review of critical components that theory, actual individual experience, and the study of many existing techniques all have demonstrated and confirmed reveals several guidelines.

A venture organization should be independent, set up to develop new businesses aggressively and with total commitment by the highest level of management. It should be organized to take advantage of entrepreneurs in an open climate, not to contain them for better control. It should be unencumbered by long decision processes, and should operate as free from administrative management as possible, permitting direct communication between the incipient entrepreneurs and all levels of corporate management. It should be self-supporting, self-motivated, and dynamic, separated from the search function with a minimum of peripheral staff, study, or reporting tasks not directly related to developing a viable, profitable business.

Organizations are made up of people, and too frequently, method and control replace action and implementation. To avoid this, a well-planned, highly structured approach that continually changes the administrative and monitoring management yields the best chance for business success. It is better to have several struggling ventures manned by a few aggressive people than one massive venture, overprotected, oversupported, and subsequently overburdened with problems other than the achievement of profit goals.

4

The Search, the Screening, and the Selection

THERE are several alternatives for choosing a venture or business opportunity. The general aspects of these alternatives are established by corporate management in its descriptive statements in the long-range plans of the company. The natural bases for routes and objectives are set in various planning documents. These guide the entrepreneur through the inception stages. In cases where small or new businesses are concerned, the concise statement of goals is often indistinguishable from the choice of the venture. Where a smaller business is being expanded or a new one developed, the tendency is to set rather broad goals as weighed against the internal capabilities to achieve them. In these cases it would be reasonable and perhaps imperative to restate the goals with priorities, or according to some other confining arrangement. Specific definition of venture goals is important to organizations of all sizes. Within that context one can find several alternative approaches to business expansion through venturing. Unfortunately, one of the most commonly used methods is, even when goals are specifically delineated, by its very nature highly random and nonspecific.

Shotgun Approach

This descriptively titled method develops from a lack of planning definition. It often is the easiest route to take, since it requires a minimum of pre-action effort by the general management body. There are advantages. The minds of imaginative leaders work best when unencumbered and unconfined by the boundaries of corporate policy and objectives. The philosophy following this argument is that from the outpouring of multiple and diverse ideas, some obviously excellent opportunities will be gleaned. The disadvantage is that a great deal of time, effort, and frequently money is expended before the unattractive or unacceptable concepts and suggestions are eliminated. This approach, by its very nature, is incompatible with the basic premise of proper planning set forth in the second chapter dealing with corporate planning. And it requires additional time.

Yet despite its negative aspects, in the hands of skilled professionals it provides a degree of latitude that stimulates, challenges, and expands the horizons of the corporation and of potential entrepreneurs. When handled cautiously under talented and enlightened leadership, the people engaged in the search are apt to apply more stringent and lower-risk criteria to the type of opportunity than they would if boundaries were initially placed upon them. The general result of the shotgun approach is that each searcher develops a set of limiting criteria that he uses as a basis for his search, screening, and selection. As long as these criteria are defined by him, it is an excellent facility.

The shotgun approach is not recommended for a small group or for less-experienced management and personnel. It contains an element of chance that the overall New Venture Methodology is designed to eliminate. Another important matter that should be considered is the number of ideas that may flow through the screening process. While it is a sign of aggressive effort to let management people see all the possibilities available to them, the objective of showing them only the most viable and profitable opportunities becomes subverted and the search method becomes the paramount activity rather than the results it produces.

Programmed Approach

This is considered the single best way to perform the tasks of search, screening, and selection. The plans, objectives, policies, and criteria are laid out, and they act as the perimeter of the area in which the venture group will operate. There are so many variations that can be described, however, that the seemingly simple directive to program a technique from search to selection is quickly revealed as highly complex. Several evaluation formats can be described, though they represent neither separate nor independent entities. Other factors must also be considered. Furthermore, variations within different specifically defined approaches can be incompatible or, to the extreme, contradictory. If such variations should occur, and are not recognized early by management, they will be found immediately by the operating staff and will color their performance. For example, if capital investment is limited, new ventures will be inhibited. The possibility of failure or of ventures becoming muddled and shifting, difficult to monitor and evaluate, can become a reality all to easily. In discussing alternatives, mention of the problem can be made, though it will be self-evident in some cases.

Corporate Compatibility

A venture might be desirable that has had one or more operational or philosophical interfaces with one of a company's existing business areas. This approach takes advantage of strengths within the corporate body. Through design, many organizations come to recognize a place in the business community that they fill better than anyone else. To capitalize on this is a logical and oftentimes successful route to new business. One should still distinguish between such a venture and a routine extension of existing business. The definition of *innovation* rather than *product improvement* indicates that some new and unexplored or underutilized data, product, or vehicle might be involved. When one object of the programmed approach is to insure substantial interaction with existing business, an agreed point of departure between the supportive, new-product-oriented suboperation within an operating division and the venture group must be made early. Aside from any intergroup controversy that might occur, a casual duplication or dual and conflicting solutions to the same problem might develop. These need not stifle the venture in a corporation in which competition and alternate choices are healthy, but the situation can seriously affect the venture group's progress. The single and most overwhelming disadvantage of this approach lies in definition, or lack of one, for compatibility between a company and a potential venture activity. Experience shows that in any organization of consequence, there are people or groups who will lay claim to, or be assigned, a position of expertise. They may contribute nothing but criticism. On the other hand, either for convenience or debate in support of their choice of a business opportunity, they always manage to find some evidence of corporate strength. Later on, it is all too frequently determined that the points were more significant in their deficiencies than their potentially advantageous effects. Some of the following variations on the programmed approach might also be classified as compatible, but by definition they avoid the aforementioned pitfalls.

Raw Materials Source

The materials requirements as a starting point—or, in the case of a service business, the manpower needed—carries a great deal of weight in major business management circles. Many people have recognized that it is frequently more beneficial to consider the starting position somewhere up the ladder from a crude or rudimentary point, as alluded to in the section on foward integration. It also has been evident that the basic supplier, who superficially controls the starting materials that ultimately find their way into consumables, gathers the lowest profit margin. Competition among the so-called commodity items is severe, and the pressure from large users for backward integration of their activities is constant. It would then be incumbent upon a company that is primarily a supplier of raw materials to exploit its own position. The venture group might be involved only in business opportunities that would result in the increased or more profitable use of its materials. This is not necessarily a limited involvement since a unique conversion of a material or a totally new market concept could be developed. It is necessary to distinguish between the continuous efforts of the ongoing business in the quest to improve sales or profits based on present capabilities, and the goals of the venturers. Whereas this approach to make better use of a raw-materials source is highly desirable from the corporate view if success is achieved, its inverted philosophy (compared, for instance, to filling market need) is often beyond solution without in-depth research and development, without a great expenditure of time and money, or without an internal commitment to challenge present major users.

Special Operational Fields

Many companies want to become or remain the leader in a specific field in which they consider themselves, or are considered by related businesses, to be strong. Even in companies where this may seem specious, the intent is real and the need to venture in special areas is important. The reputation, name, or impression the corporate body lends to the venture is advantageous, as is the reluctance of competition to meet the new entry head on in the marketplace. While the value of these factors should not be minimized, it is equally important to realize that they are but individual elements among many of the driving forces needed to achieve success. Too frequently the competition does not share the concern about coincidental products or marketing, or the consumer is less impressed by the producer and his name than by the product or service. The negativism expressed here concerning the value of a name may be exaggerated, but it is presented this way to reinforce awareness of the need for proper evaluation of these as well as other factors. Despite the pros and cons regarding the field of specialty in which a company is believed to be esteemed, the venture must still enter this area if that is the direction set by the corporation. There should be no reluctance to follow its directives, since opportunity still exists and the challenge must be to search, screen, and select within the confines of this policy.

Market Capability

It is quite simple to determine and demonstrate the area in which an organization has marketing qualifications. Its current product lines are known and customers can be categorized. The choice made by management in its statement of objectives could limit the company to those areas that can take advantage of the existing market staff or customer contacts. It would be more appropriate to allow some latitude in extending the customer list and expanding the sales force. Limiting venture objectives could create the problem of how to separate venture efforts from the normal product and/or service growth projected in the long-range plans of the present operation. The same type of problem exists in the case of the company that might upgrade raw materials to acquire new business. It is best to clearly separate the goals of the operational and venture organizations to avoid those problems when conflict can occur. The virtue of using marketing capabilities above others is that it permits a broader range of opportunities. Frequently the sales force, from management to line salesman, is the venture team's greatest ally. The field needs new products to stimulate growth in sales for all products. The salesmen are closest to this need and are more than willing to supply data from customers to help find solutions to these problems. Many treatises on new-product development cover the market-capability approach in detail because it has proved to be among the most successful. In New Venture Methodology it has less impact, since new marketing organizations are anticipated. In any case, the method should not be minimized considering the effect it could have in demonstrating early success.

Corporate Edict

A few comments can be made about this, though the word *edict* is effective in its candor. When corporate management decides that venture activity is to be initiated in a certain area of its choosing, two things occur. Primarily, the support of management and of all levels between and peripheral to the venture group is assured, which provides a strong hand for the entrepreneur. This does not say he would not have it under other circumstances; it is just more pronounced in this case. Secondarily, the give-'im-what-he-wants attitude emerges. The prevailing feeling that the answer is known and the entrepreneur should fill in the question can be detrimental to the proper selection of an opportunity. This makes it difficult, but not necessarily intolerable. In defense of this approach, it must be realized that many times the picture is more clearly seen by management, especially when it has excellent supportive data, good planning, and an enlightened overview of industrial and business trends. This holds true especially in smaller companies. The technique requires the same commitment as any venture, but it tends to get the desired commitment for the wrong reasons.

Totally New Business Entity

Ideally, flexibility in the quest of venture opportunities is greatest when a business is sought that is totally new to the company. But the theory that a new business development is most desirable has its pitfalls. The larger the corporate body, the more likely it is that any venture chosen has a relationship with some area of corporate interest or operation. In a small company this is less likely, however; the concept of a totally new business may be too grandiose. The obvious compromise is to select business opportunities that are not, by design, an extension of current capabilities, but do take advantage of the corporate background. It would appear that even those opportunities recognized as not totally new eventually require an independent organization to develop them. This occurs even when imaginative imitation shapes the opportunity.

New Venture Methodology can function as a means of entering a new area. Opting to create a new business allows a wide range of choice, but in screening and selection, factors affecting compatibility and strength will always be considered. The greatest difficulty in assigning only totally new entities to venture responsibility is that reliance on corporate capabilities is denied. This statement should never be categorical, since exceptions never cease to arise. Another important problem with totally new areas is that the venture can lack direction. Apparently good opportunities are sometimes rejected because they are too new, too foreign, or too diverse. In the best situations, flexibility is maximized or optimized, allowing a combination of various approaches.

Fiscal Determination

The financial basis for choosing a venture opportunity can be superimposed on all the preceding alternatives. Here the emphasis is on a monetary boundary in the search. There are published examples of companies that look only for opportunities of significant size with potential in the multimillion-dollar range. Other companies reportedly put sales ceilings of a million dollars on a mature product. At less than one million dollars in sales, the market is too small for competition to attempt to split it. In this range, the business can be comfortably handled by internal funding.

The fiscal determination does not limit the type or direction of the opportunity sought. When it is the only boundary, flexibility is great. Additional parameters may be advisable to inject more specific guidance. In fiscal determinations, dollar potentials are estimates or best guesses and tend to be described in order of magnitude, which results in greater uncertainty. Dollar estimates should therefore be judged accordingly, within a time framework.

The programmed approach includes several possibilities. The use of one or more of these methods not only can be helpful to the venture leader and analyst, but will yield more acceptable opportunities and a greater chance of their success.

Technical Means Versus Market Need

The best approach for a new business opportunity remains a choice that must ultimately be made by the individual organization. Two different avenues are frequently discussed concerning new-product development. One way has in-hand technology which has the capability of doing some unidentified job as its starting point.

Technical Means

The technical route to new business may include an invention, either internally or externally generated, an innovation, or an imaginative though imitative entry into the marketplace. Any of these makes a good starting point, and frequently originates new products. It is the simplest way to approach the problems of new ventures as well. The chance of success in the market when one has no solutions to any known problem, but merely a novel technological development, is minimal. Although this is obvious, many hope to find uses for such a development as a program progresses. To consider a venture without an established technical capability is foolhardy. This is not to suggest that it should be the starting point, but that the lack of it could cause an early rejection. The problem lies in making a judgment about the current state of the technology and which problem it will solve. When further data, modification of the technology, or demonstration of it is required, it is better handled in a directed research or development program implemented outside the venture group. The word *judgment* precludes any dogma that might be associated with these recommendations. What is needed is a specific recognition of the degree and depth of the technological capability. But by itself it is hollow without a consideration of the market need.

Market Need

The alternate approach is to begin with a market need. It is simple and almost glib to state that one should start with a market need. This is without doubt an excellent goal, a highly desirable attitude, and, in theory, the ultimate in good sense. The major problem here is to define that need. In considering the market need, who is to determine that it exists and what form it takes? Several sources are available. There are the experts, those who consult, plan, study markets, sell in specific markets, manage, invent, and so on. The point is that expertise does not lie in one segment of the business community. There are too many clever, humorous, tragic, and interesting stories of men who rejected outstanding technical contributions because in their judgment there was no market need. For example, the telephone and xerography were not initially accepted by those closest to the very need these inventions eventually fulfilled. Other examples of improper definition of a need, such as failure to distinguish between need and desire, have led to poor choices of potential opportunity.

Market needs change, often rapidly, and early rather than late recognition of that can yield the difference between success and failure. There are obvious advantages in finding a market need first and then devising a technical means of filling it. Initial sales success is enhanced, growth is almost guaranteed, and price is less critical with the possibility of increased profits. The adverse effect may be equally obvious, and it is surely far more devastating. The problem is well defined, the need is delineated, and the means of meeting it is then sought. If that technical means is not reasonable or possible, or requires a major breakthrough, and the time needed to reach a solution is unreasonably extended, what appeared to be a business opportunity may disintegrate. Finding a cure for cancer is a good case in point. The need is well stated, the market is readily defined, and the social and humane aspects hold far greater value than the economic implications. As a business opportunity, it would be discouraging, simply by virtue of the lack of a technical breakthrough. The importance of this shortcoming is evident when one realizes that the government is the only organization large enough to substantially fund work to find a solution.

In conclusion, these courses are neither independent nor incompatible. Filling the market need, however important and obvious it is, requires technical implementation. Conversely, having the capability to solve a nonproblem is certainly of no commercial value. To some degree, a market can always be found for the unique invention with no existing market, and accommodation can be made for the technology that creates a novel market. When we deal with high-order needs in an affluent society, these factors are dynamic and temporary. The electric carving knife fits the former description and the well-known hoola hoop the latter. Where need and means are concerned, integration is the best answer. The venture search may start from either base, but continual mingling of market needs and technical means is required. The mental processes of the entrepreneurial integrator play a critical role in these initial phases of search, screening, and selection. Later in the venture process, analysts will categorize need and means, and quantitative descriptions will be developed for them. At this stage much reliance must be placed on intuition, imagination, and integration of present knowledge. Means and needs are integral and inseparable.

Search for Venture Opportunities

This section will deal with finding sources of potential opportunities. It is well recognized that search should be a responsibility of everyone in the organization. Planning and market research can make important contributions. The major consideration is that the search for opportunities not be an idle activity. Therefore, responsibility should finally reside in some individual or group. Whereas every operating and staff department feels the need to support its own interests, their finds, however superfluous, should be welcomed by the venture personnel. In many cases, venture people can also route to others opportunities that they recognize as more appropriate for someone else. In any ongoing search, a personal liaison between the venture group and other segments of the company should be set up for smooth communications. In larger organizations, it is mandatory that this task be assigned to venture groups, with open communications sanctioned by everyone.

There are many sources of the four I's (*idea, invention, innovation, improvement*) that comprise an opportunity. Following are descriptions of as many of these as are practical to relate. They derive from internal and external sources, the former often an indirect extension of the latter. Such duplication can be helpful and should result in more complete and effective coverage of the field.

External Sources

In the past there has been a disparity between internal and external sources. The latter have been more prolific and successful. But now this gap is closing through better-controlled and more modern venture management techniques. Outside organizations still represent a good source of opportunity. The first consideration might be the U.S. government with its multitude of branches and subdivisions.

United States government	Search companies (technological,
Private foundations	acquisitions, product)
Public institutions	Research and management organizations
Colleges and universities	Foreign trade commissions
Research institutes	Advertising agencies
Information and service groups	Investment banking
Trade associations	Corporations (United States
State and local government	and foreign)

There is no way to blanket sources from the U.S. government. Such pamphlets as the *Patent Gazette* are most helpful. Companies and individuals can have their names put on mailing lists from the Superintendent of Documents, the publisher for the federal government. Because of numerous possibilities, it is necessary to limit oneself to those reviews that might have direct relevance. This points up the need for multiple search centers within a corporate body. Private foundations often require a personal contact for best results. Where nonobligatory contributions are made, the entrée is generally easier. Public institutions such as hospitals can be approached on a random basis where applicable. Institutions often mail out their house organs for a nominal cost. It is recommended that colleges or universities be chosen selectively; strong support from a few is far superior to general coverage that is ineffectively pursued.

Research institutes vary in their relationships with private industry. This is an individual matter and should be handled as such. Contracts with information and service groups like American Management Association, Stanford Research Institute, and Predicasts can be most fruitful and supply a depth of source material not available internally. Trade associations can be helpful within the limits of their specialties. Engaging search companies is quite acceptable if they are given a proper definition of the objectives and the intent to act on their findings is strong and committed. Market research organizations under project direction can be invaluable for their fresh views and alternate approaches. Trade commissions, investment bankers, and advertising agencies work well where a contact exists or a specific problem or area to investigate is recognized.

The use of information from other corporations requires a deeper involvement than the others. Here, a degree of commitment, certain legal ramifications, and careful negotiations can be inherent in the discussions and contacts. However, their house organs, or in some cases their spin-off staff, are readily available, directly or at some nominal fee. Again, the justification for time and expenditure must be a desire to proceed with a find that results from such contacts.

Printed Matter

The biggest problem with this source of information is the magazine syndrome. A clever reporter or public relations man whose words stimulate an idea recessed in the mind of the reader can activate some excessively time-consuming games. Isolated facts might spell new opportunity, but chances are the cost will eventually be high, and many such opportunities will not reach fruition. A list of literature sources follows.

Technical journals
Trade journals
Professional magazines
Consumer magazines
Newsprint
Corporate publications and mailouts, annual reports
Patents and abstracts
Advertisements
New products reports
Business directories
Library reviews
Convention papers and technical presentations

Individuals

People are the best single source for well-thought-out and well-integrated opportunities. Many people carry around pet projects or composite proposals in their heads, and most are more than willing to discuss them. A caution of legal entanglement is apropos, however, and *caveat emptor* should be kept in mind on hearing each disclosure. People may present them with the utmost sincerity, but this is no substitute for your best judgment and analytical appraisal. Individual sources include those in the following list.

Entrepreneurs
Inventors
Suppliers
Customers and customers' customers
Consultants
Professional contacts
Technology brokers
Patent agents
People in the previously listed organizations
Investment and financial specialists

The world around us is full of potential opportunity sources, and it is important first to determine which are most applicable to present requirements and objectives.

Internal Sources

Many sources are available in each organization, according to its complexity. Ideally, the primary internal source is the new-ventures group, which, through its own talents, contacts, and ferreting, will produce a continuous flow of good items worth screening. But one can also look to the other general corporate functions common to most companies.

Sales organization. The sales force (or forces in divisionalized and departmentalized companies) serves as an excellent source through good reporting on customer needs, new and potential customer requests, applications, problems, and suggestions. The inquiries of purchasing agents, manufacturing engineers, distributors, and prospective users elicit additional data. These men and their management meet competition head-on daily, and they are familiar with products that affect them directly as well as with changes taking place in a competitor's line, moves being made by companies producing allied products, and tests or queries on substitute products. They sometimes overreact, and many of the items reported are not venture opportunities. This should not be allowed to dampen the enthusiasm of the sales force, however, and the analyst should keep these lines of communication open.

Product groups. The manufacturing operation, often viewed as mundane in its contribution to this area, is too frequently underestimated. It is granted that this function is vested with the task of producing according to plan at minimum cost, which in itself is a consuming problem. Despite this, those in manufacturing also come in contact with a set of people who can help give birth to new opportunities. Their suppliers of raw materials, equipment, and miscellaneous services represent a unique set of contacts that the sales force does not meet. Their sensitivity to product change, resulting from their first-hand view of existing products, can be substantial.

Technical staff. We readily recognize the roles that research and development and engineering can play as idea sources. This should not be minimized, although it is self-evident in most cases and has been discussed thoroughly in management and technical publications. Staff services are a fertile source of ideas. The major consideration is how to arrange a flow from the various talents in this category without its becoming a full-time task. Whereas personal contact appears to be the best route, a more formal, written communications system in which responses are required will prove to be the single most desirable means for eliciting ideas.

Management. Finally, we shall consider management as a supplier of information to the search team. There is a tendency among search teams to give special credence to management, generally because of failure to recognize corporate goals. Once these are in proper perspective, management's contribution can be handled as part of the routine or flexible procedure that the searcher has developed to integrate and screen.

Screening

The screening process is not only one of the most critical operations, it is also the most complicated judgment task. Potential opportunities from the sources discussed must first be read and understood. This simple statement represents a first-order requirement, and all too frequently it is not adhered to with the determined firmness necessary. Because of the diversity of opportunities with which the venture searcher may be bombarded, the difficulties in critically and openly reading and understanding the proposals cannot be understated.

One measure to ease the load on the screening analyst is to develop a dynamic and clean system for screening. What is described here is not a proposed system but an outline that could be used to develop one. The initial step is to list the few questions that relate directly to the appropriate go, no-go criteria for an acceptable business opportunity. At this point, the planning done at various levels of management pays off. Some criteria from these plans, if not met, would eliminate the suggestion from further consideration. When a no-go situation arises, the best approach is to get at least one independent opinion that the judgment is correct, if only in the most informal context or discussion. The second step for acceptable concepts is to define, as quantitatively as possible, the next group of solutions needed. Finally, some additional data might be highly desirable before committing to a selection, information more general in nature requiring intuition, a best guess, or indirect analysis.

Market Considerations

There are several categories of screening, and a discussion of them is usually best started with the market consideration. Market size, the venture's relation to a need, and the physical location of the market are some aspects to study. Methods of distribution and sales, geographic influences, and customer concentrations provide information for the initial screening. Several aspects of the market, such as its growth or nongrowth characteristics, product newness to the market, and cyclical or unstable nature, all play a role.

There are still other sources of information that can be critical to evaluation, depending on the organization using them. These might include inventory practices, economic indices, reputation, pricing and its history, service requirements, segmentations or fragmentations, reciprocity, internal use, export possibilities, and dominant forces in the market or the economy. Competition, in its broadest interpretation, should be considered as well. Some superficial market identification, characterization, and structure, and sales capabilities for the product can be made by the analyst.

Other factors to take into account are the possibility of expansions, modifications, methods, profit margin, overcrowding, overproduction, customer relationships and migrations, and new competition arising out of obvious strengths in other companies. A checklist can encompass any or all of these, as well as additional items deemed important by the analyst. Answers must be readily available, although a complete and detailed job is not sought or achieved. (This is still an elementary stage, not the analysis.) Proper weight in terms of time and effort must be afforded each suggested opportunity.

Marketing and merchandising are also part of the screening process. Some of the factors are:

Market opportunity, potential, and penetration
Earnings possibilities
Market forecasts
Industry and market interest
Patterns of product flow
Existing sales forces and customers
Advertising and promotion requirements

Product Considerations

Manufacturing can be covered in sufficient detail to get an order-of-magnitude cost of investment over the early life of the project. Some of the following are worthy of inclusion.

Available facilities and processes
Space, equipment, and design needs
Raw material availability and cost
Purchasing, leverage
Competition's approaches
Maintenance, waste, and safety

Financial information on production costs might be sketchy at this point. While estimates of sales and costs of sales and production would be vague and border on worthlessness, early thought about them is helpful. If one thinks in terms of incremental costs, profit potentials, dollar growths, cash flow, dollar recovery, long-term prospects, price erosions, and net investment during this stage, later analysis is less likely to indicate a startling reversal of the selection decisions.

Three additional areas to consider are the product(s) or service involved, its manufacture in terms of process definition, and the inherent technology. Here are some facets of the screening stage applicable under specific circumstances:

Product
  Imitative or new
  Life cycle and wearout
  Deficiencies and advantages
  Properties, required and desired
  Codes, restrictions, and approvals
  Type of consumer

Testing and acceptability
Legal ramifications
Process
    Reliability and yield
    Development needed
    Capacity and timing
    Plant selection and design
    Basic cost
    Competitive and alternate methods
Technology
    Existing knowledge
    Laboratory requirements
    Patents, publications, licenses
    Rate of obsolescence
    Basic obstacles
    Consultants

The important factor in the whole screening process is to choose proper areas of interest to the company, to the venture analyst, and to the decision makers. The decision is frequently made by the analyst through his own mental integration of known information and the predefined criteria.

The reason for the many components listed in this chapter is to allow a wide range of possibilities from which to choose. Once this is provided and the amount and criticality of the data are determined, screening becomes less subjective and more objective. In that it is more than just desirable to be objective, and the time allotted to accept concepts, proposals, and opportunities from the various sources and then to screen them is limited, boundaries must be set on the criteria. These should be chosen according to the criteria necessary to make a reasonable selection. Further data are always attractive and often beneficial, but they may have no effect on the decision-making process. Therefore it is best to pick the criteria required to make a quick and, one hopes, accurate decision to analyze further or reject the source proposal.

While relatively little space has been devoted to screening, it should be recognized that its relationship to selection is close to inseparable. In screening, we dealt with the type of question to be considered, the extent of detail required, and the obvious signs of rejection. This screening is actually preparation for the selection process, which occurs after the first positive indications are developed that a viable opportunity might exist. Selection is a more quantitative approach, taking the information based on screening criteria and putting it into a more formal document. This is a combination document designed to locate any anomalies missed in screening, to determine the relative value of an opportunity (and hence its priority), and to allow selection of the best choices for further action.

It is assumed for purposes of ready demonstration that certain items come to the venture group for screening through external search or unsolicited corporate activities. Of these, a certain number might be too formative for screening, though this should be determined in the first step of screening. Another factor to assess might be whether the product is innovative. A new product, process, or service may be the only possible type of venture acceptable to general management as stated in its plans and policies. The personal judgment of the individual analyst comes into play at this stage. He must sense some excitement generated by the concept or opportunity. His interpretation, influenced by personal likes and dislikes, is necessary, and it is for this reason that only carefully chosen people, unencumbered by an individualized, unitary management, are going to yield successful performance.

Other significant questions crop up, such as, "Is there presently a market, is there one in the foreseeable future, is the competition great, are we too late, is it worth the cost predicted, do other alternatives take priority over use, and is the time right?" Less subjective questions for determining if further evaluation is necessary include, for example, "Does it meet our corporate plans and objectives, does it compete with present operations, is it large enough to have impact on our corporation, can we make a short-term profit, and is the growth obviously above average?" When such questions determined by the analyst evoke *yes* answers, even based on spurious data and limited information, the second stage of screening and the subsequent selection phase are undertaken.

Approaches to Screening

These three suggested approaches can undoubtedly be refined, modified, and tailored to the individual need. The choice of each is based on some fundamental concepts and can be used only as comparative tools, not as absolute, independent ratings. The most difficult job is to design them to work for one's own use, and probably no other person will devise a similar technique. It should, however, be sufficiently broad, clear, and easy to use, and should be insensitive to minor readjustments. In the absence of any of the answers, either the ratings or confidence levels should be obvious estimates or they should make up a small enough part of the whole to cause little change in the decision or profile if it is altered on the basis of new information.

When additional data are obtained, the entire result will necessarily change, and it should if the new data are critical to the decision and diverge from original intelligence.

Profile technique. Figure 17 charts a profile of a product. The numbers at the column heads represent the criteria by which the product is rated. Criteria for selection of a venture opportunity should be listed in order of decreasing importance and should remain constant. As the venture analyst or group becomes more sophisticated, changes in these headings can be made. A limit of 10 to 15 criteria is advisable because of the time factor in carrying out the procedure for each suggested opportunity that passes initial screening. The rating is an arbitrary scale, here shown as A to E. The A stands for excellent or superior whereas the E means marginal. One must assume that any rating below marginal is sufficient reason for immediate rejection. If it is not sufficient reason, one should reevaluate the criteria since the value of the individual criterion is obviously small and perhaps insignificant. In fact, this is a good point to consider when choosing criteria. If the proposal must rate above marginal to be selected, the criterion is a good one. It's a mistake to get bogged down in trivial items or make selections on the basis of fallacious criteria.

The chart developed from this technique can then be translated to a graphic profile. The comparison, by using overlays, is easily made

Figure 17. Product profile criteria in descending order of importance.

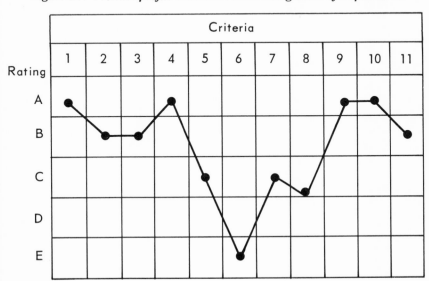

but hard to judge. To distinguish between a profile that is constant across the criteria at a median level and ones that are irregular, high in initial criteria but diminishing later, the converse of that, or some other indescribable shape, is a herculean task. This is the reason for using a more quantitative approach. As evaluations become more quantitative, criteria become more specialized and are less applicable across a multitude of situations. Although comparison of venture profiles can show differences, it is better to combine them with the following methods for better results.

Comparative rating. A technique that approximates a number of proposed analyses is recommended for use in comparative rating. Criteria are listed in their order of importance but broken into subgroups for clarification. For example, under criterion 1 in Figure 18, marketing is the most important item. It is weighted 9 on a 1-to-10 scale. The components of marketing are described as a direct sales force, existing customers, and advertising expertise. Each would be equally assigned one-third of the total, or a value of 3. Where there are no minor components, the criterion takes on full weighting. The opportunity under evaluation is then assigned numerical ratings from 1 to 10 for each criterion, the higher number being the better score. The product of the weight times the rating gives a score for each criterion, and the sum of them all yields a final number used for comparison. This method's shortcoming is that it gives the impression of precision, while it still may require many subjective judgments. It does not, by the summation figure, describe problem areas, though problems may be evident in the individual criteria. It is a helpful tool since it allows the combination of criteria into coherent groupings, and subtotals can be used for improved meaning and interpretation.

While rating the opportunity, evaluation of competition can be made. Relative judgments may show where and to what extent there are advantages or delinquencies. Not too much stock should be placed in the differences unless they are large, easily explained by examining individual criteria, and/or they have been subjected to a variance analysis of some type. That would not appear to be worth the trouble at this point in screening and selection, since analysis will follow that uses the kind of detail needed for making decisions about economic outlays. The other portion of Figure 18 demonstrates that alternate concepts can be compared as well. This could be an alternate choice, or a suspected market entry by competition. The same holds true in estimating this potential and in attempting to draw too precise a conclusion. The input is probably highly intuitive, and gives the analyst a look at his own opinions. Numbers are attractive, and there is a ten-

Figure 18. Comparative rating system.

Criteria	Weight	Ratings					
		Opportunity	Product	Competition	Product	Alternative	Product
Major Criterion 1							
Minor Segment	3	5	15	6	18	5	15
Minor Segment	3	5	15	4	12	2	6
Minor Segment	3	9	27	8	24	8	24
Major Criterion 2							
Minor Segment	4	3	12	4	16	6	24
Minor Segment	4	7	28	5	20	6	24
Major Criterion 3	7	7	49	5	35	6	42
Major Criterion 4	7	6	42	7	49	2	14
Major Criterion 5							
Minor Segment	2	8	16	3	6	4	8
Minor Segment	2	8	16	4	8	5	10
Minor Segment	1	2	2	3	3	4	4
Minor Segment	1	5	5	5	5	5	5
Summation			227		196		176

dency to relegate the results to a position of honor. But this could be disastrous to a sound decision. The results should be recognized as guidelines only.

Confidence level. The use of confidence-level rating as shown in Figure 19 is somewhat better in some respects than the comparative system, but it has problems of its own. Weighting the criteria is the same, but the rating for each criterion cannot be too exact. This allows, and requires, a bit more subjectivity using high, medium, and low ratings. The numbers 10, 5, and 1 were assigned respectively to each level, though any value could be used for facile arithmetic and clear meaning. The key to this approach is the confidence that the analyst has in the data proposed to him or obtained from his general sources. Necessarily, the high, medium, and low ratings for the opportunity score are the best guesses in some cases, so one is then rating the guesses. If there is a low-confidence figure for a highly weighted criterion, it is necessary to find a better opportunity or to question whether the opportunity is in fact decent and acceptable. It is imperative to have a reasonable level of confidence in an opportunity before selecting it, which this approach insures by forcing an evaluation of confidence. The product of the weighting, the score, and the confidence assigns a value to each criterion. The summation is a nondimensional number that can be used for comparison or selection, or both.

Selection

Use of Scoring Techniques

What is a good score? How do you make the selection? These are appropriate questions that defy a simple answer. The best indications are general in nature and refer to some techniques that must be developed by the individual to determine the minimum level of acceptance. It was already stated that any criterion that rates zero or below should be sufficient to reject an apparently marginal opportunity. Sometimes the comparative rating may show that competition rates zero in a critical criterion and yet survives in the marketplace. This kind of anomaly does occur, and when the problem caused by the deficiency in the existing product is solved by a new product, the existing product is rendered obsolete. This is a good sign, and should be especially noted for important consideration. It might also indicate that a criterion has been misstated. Further, a low confidence-level rating is tantamount to dismissing the potential opportunity. At this

Figure 19. Confidence level.

Criteria	Weight	Opportunity score High 10	Opportunity score Medium 5	Opportunity score Low 1	Confidence High 10	Confidence Medium 5	Confidence Low 1	Product
Major Criterion 1								
Minor Segment	3		✓		✓			150
Minor Segment	3		✓		✓			150
Minor Segment	3	✓				✓		150
Major Criterion 2								
Minor Segment	4			✓	✓			40
Minor Segment	4	✓				✓		200
Major Criterion 3	7	✓			✓			700
Major Criterion 4	7		✓			✓		175
Major Criterion 5								
Minor Segment	2	✓					✓	20
Minor Segment	2	✓			✓			200
Minor Segment	1			✓	✓			10
Minor Segment	1		✓			✓		25
Summation								1820

point some expert advice may be needed, if all other segments look good.

The ideal result would be a straight-line profile chart, rating all criteria as excellent. Too many C's would be suspect, though the business opportunity may be reasonable for a particular company. If a fourth of the criteria are D's or a tenth are E's, it would be advisable to look for a better opportunity. Since the object of venturing is to improve the chances of success, at less cost, in less time, look for those prospects that yield only A's and B's unless the criteria, set by corporate plans and policy, are so tight and stringent as to be overly confining and demanding.

Once a base line for a successful opportunity has been worked out in the comparative rating, venture selection should be related to that base. Experience with any number of commercial products chosen at random lends some insight. It is hard to put oneself in the right place at the right time with all the correct information available, but it is possible to make best estimates. Results show that had certain successfully marketed products been scored by the comparative rating procedure before they went to market, a score of 75 on a 100-point base would have been the lowest found. This affirms that three-quarters of the potential point value should be achieved for the best chance of success. In cases in which more marginal opportunities are acceptable, two-thirds might suffice. The penalty, however, is not generally less success but a greater possibility for failure. In ventures in which risk may be more acceptable, this stage is not the time to take it. In such cases an 80 on a 100 base would be the recommended value for selection. The succeeding analysis will justify the conservative basis for selection by rewarding both the analyst and his company with not only better opportunities but successful ones. Analysis is a costly step in time and money, and should be used only for prime selections.

Confidence-level values are even more difficult to assess. The numerical difference between a 10-weighted criterion scored medium in confidence and the identically weighted criterion with a high confidence score is a factor of 2 on the scale (10, 5, 1) shown in Figure 18. Even when a 3, 2, 1 scale is used, a 50 percent difference occurs. The result is large variances with small apparent changes in valuation. On the basis of the 10, 5, 1 scale for the opportunity score and confidence levels, a 60- to 70-fold increase over the total weighting value in the first column is anticipated for good opportunities. At 60 times the overall weighting, the selection could be marginal for further analysis of the opportunity. For venture opportunities of significant value, no low ratings of either type would be acceptable, and at least one-half the weighting of criteria should be among the more important factors.

The searching, screening, and selection stages lead to the analysis of a chosen potential opportunity. Searching should be as broad as reasonable, screening as time-conserving as possible, and selection as critical and demanding as practical. The time spent on good selection of opportunities is worthwhile, accomplishing two objectives: only good opportunities are analyzed in depth, and only excellent ones are venture-directed into successful, profitable commercialization.

5

The Analysis

THE preceding chapters have indicated that new-venture management, using New Venture Methodology, is an extension of prior knowledge supplemented by modern business techniques. According to this method, each company chooses and adjusts those techniques to attain its objective of finding and using an approach that will help the company to achieve growth by taking advantage of business opportunities quickly, at the lowest cost in manpower, dollars, and time, and with minimum risk. Planning must be done in sufficient detail to avoid choosing an opportunity of apparent excellence only to discover that corporate management has no intention of funding a venture in the chosen areas or market. The group that implements these objectives is important to ultimate success in that committed people are required. Both these observations are simplifications, but they lay the groundwork for beginning to look for the proper opportunity. The search can be complex or simple, depending on the searcher and the objectives. Sources are plentiful, and the major imperative is to narrow the field and to focus only on those areas that can prove fruitful. Screening is the first real challenge to the entrepreneur. A quick survey of suggested opportunities, using qualitative and some partially quantitative measures, results in the selection of a few good-looking opportunities. The judgment and integration of the entire available data are in the hands of the analyst who will select attractive opportunities and then justify his choice.

This stage of the venture method should be subjected to a critical review by immediate venture management. The conclusions of the analyst should also be part of an oral report to the next-higher level of administrative management to be sure the goals are known and accepted and that no objection, obvious or hidden, is overlooked. Often the only requirements are a tacit agreement from management and the potential venture leader's desire to proceed. Despite the analyst's willingness to proceed, to do so unilaterally is dangerous. A reiteration of management's concurrence and commitment is necessary. This point marks a good time to recognize the more time-consuming and frequently manpower-requiring aspects of running an analysis. If there is no formal document that spells out the objectives, facilities, money, and personnel needs, the analysis can falter and the goals go unachieved.

Management Commitment

Through the initial selection stage, one man has been operating individually under a small budget. When a selection is made and confirmed, the team enters the picture. In view of the need for a group with diverse capabilities to study and follow the venture, an increased expenditure of money and time is in order. For 60 to 90 days, the analyst, now the leader, and his appointed team will devote full time and energies to their single objective. This should only be done with the complete concurrence and blessings of the management chain. If the venture manager reports at the highest level, a most desirable factor, the chief operating officer will have been informed of the expanded plan and his approval given. Commitment is complete and the analysis phases are initiated.

Analysis Segments

Analysis can be as detailed and sophisticated as time allows and opportunity demands. Since analysis is a continuing effort from this point forward, at no time are there too few data and never is the task complete. The significance of these statements becomes obvious as the components of analysis are discussed. The various portions of the analysis have been segregated into six sections: (1) technical, (2) engineering, (3) manufacturing, (4) market and sales, (5) financial, and (6) legal. We will examine them in that order, with emphasis on the tools rather than the questions to be asked and answered, which may vary from situation to situation. Not every possible analytical aspect has been included; each case will direct the facets to be incorporated and influence how they are tailored.

Technical Analysis

There are many factors in the technical analysis that duplicate or at least overlap the manufacturing and market analyses. This is true of all the analyses, and although they can be handled independently, the venture leader coordinates the interchange of information within his team to insure consistency, avoid duplication of effort, and stimulate communication and efficient data collection among team members.

The technical analysis can take several forms. One is the verbalization of the technical feasibility. Many questions could be designed to help make such a determination. A concise response helps to define the degree of effort that might be required to reach the proper level of acceptable technical feasibility. Another tool is the generalized rating system, which, as was pointed out in the discussion on screening and selection, might range from a simple numerical rating to a sophisticated formulation that assigns quantitative values and measures venture worth. The final evaluation for feasibility is a technical evaluation form that encompasses both of the former methods with implementation times, economic considerations, and the venture's projected effect on the general techno-business climate and environment.

Verbalization approach. The checklist is a good device for studying the technical aspects of a new product, as in the accompanying model. In the discussions on various possibilities for business opportunity, the idea, invention, innovation, and improvement sequence was covered. Relating to this, the first question might concern the newness of the product. There is no fault to be found with locating an opportunity by utilizing imaginative imitation, but it should be recognized for what it is. The point of this checklist query is to reveal just how the opportunity is defined. For the planning of time and effort, it is necessary to know whether the product is new or imitative, whether it is an original idea or technical innovation, and whether the analyst really believes that it possesses those features reported to him by others. Hearsay enters into many analysis decisions, but wherever possible, recognition and justification or corroboration are desired. Judgment questions to determine the item's chances for success and acceptance, its patentability or any other proprietary aspects, its position in the development cycle, and its uniqueness in the present market are recommended for further exploration of technical viability. Frequently data will be difficult to derive or obtain, so it is helpful to identify similar markets or extensions of existing markets and technologies.

Question 6 on the checklist concerns the degree of product variation and descriptions within the product line. The converse of that is equally important, when a very rigid or restricted need or capability exists. The response to this question eventually indicates the need for further technical efforts. These should supply the market analysis with appropriate considerations.

When it can be defined, the extent of previous research, development, engineering, or technical evaluation of the product should be determined. These data will be most helpful for later financial analysis. Recognition in trade and technical literature of the product's competitive activity serves several purposes. For one thing, it demon-

---

Checklist for Technical Analysis

1. Is it a new product or product concept? What are its chances for technical success and acceptance?
2. Is it patented by us, or is it proprietary?
3. Is it in the early or mature stages of development?
4. Is it new to the marketplace?
5. Is it an extension or innovation related to an existing market?
6. Is it single-line or multiphasic (does it come in varied sizes, shapes, colors, and so on)?
7. Is our investment extensive?
8. Is there indication of competitive activity?
9. Are the raw materials available? Do we have the proper skills and talents available?
10. Are there formidable development problems ahead?
11. What is the product life cycle?
12. What is the use life?
13. Is new technology following?
14. Does it need technical service?
15. Does it require in-depth technical support?
16. Can it be reproduced?
17. Has it been produced outside the laboratory?
18. Can specifications be drawn?
19. Are end-use properties defined and proved?
20. Are specialists required for its use?
21. Are government approvals required, and have they been obtained?
22. Has the need been recognized and defined?
23. Are research reports written or in process?
24. Are there champions for this in the technical department?

strates that other firms also recognize the opportunity. Then the necessity for rapid action becomes apparent, and projected early competition in pricing and other factors can be considered with proper emphasis.

The questions dealing with the product—what materials should go into it, formidable problems still unsolved, its potential useful life, and its projected life cycle—are but a few of those to which the analyst addresses himself. The remainder of the questions are self-explanatory. Some are more important than others, and no weighting has been given individual questions. When answers are sought and developed, the relative importance of the questions will then become most apparent. When government approval is required, as by a Food and Drug Administration testing program, it is heavily weighted because of the go, no-go implication. When none is needed, the question never becomes a criterion; hence it is unweighted. The last question was included for its impact value. If the answer is yes, it is a blessing. When a product is oversold by the developers, the venture people may be expected to produce the impossible. When it is undersold or umbilically fastened to the researchers, there may be a problem in convincing them to part with it, or persuading management to accept the analyst's word that it is ready. Friction can develop in trying to solve these dilemmas. With the measures taken to list the factors in doubt, a new degree of familiarization can occur. The responses, whether qualitative or quantitative, give added dimension to the analysis. From these preliminary deductions, the introduction to comparative analysis with some numerical base is made rather smoothly.

State of value added. Figure 20 shows an example of an approach to technical analysis that stresses the value added at various development points. Rather than use a weighted value in an initial evaluation, a graphic method can be used to gain some interesting insights into the present status and future direction of the opportunity. The profile reveals which criteria are important, where operations are planned or required, and the stage of development at which the product will be utilized. The workings of the system become clearer when a hypothetical case is used. For example, if one criterion is the availability of raw materials for manufacturing the product, the profile may show that they are available in a form not readily adapted to the desired end product. In cases where certain use regulations must be met, the relative status of the material in regard to those regulations can be defined at any stage along the chain of increased product sophistication. A device may require code clearance, whereas its components may not. If the regulations are met by the final product being sold, the need for subjecting the precursor materials to such clearance is obviated. This is a simple tool for describing the value added to a raw material, but it still falls short of a quantitative tool. Like any proper representation, however, the function it serves is to lend continuity to the entire analysis. Credence for technical analysis is supported by this and other documentation.

Needs-desires rating. Another type of evaluation is a simple weighting-rating system. Similar types have been described in helping in the selection of an opportunity. The major difference in Figure 21 would be that the criteria are detailed and are segmented into needs and desires. The technical criteria are derived from the checklist questions. The weighting and rating are supplied by interviews with those persons most familiar with the product and its development. The rating is nondimensional and can only have a comparative meaning. Hence some tangible probability-of-success level must be set for each criterion and for the total.

Perhaps a better and more complete but more complex analysis would be made using the format in Figure 22. This chart integrates the criteria, their importance through weighting, their relative status

Figure 20. State of value added.

	Criteria						
	A	B	C	D	E	F	G
Total package							
Structure							
Device							
Incorporated component							
End product							
Formulated mixture							
Purified material							
Raw material							

by rating, and the confidence of the evaluator in the levels chosen. It contains both needs and desires, with appropriate weightings to distinguish between them.

A technical evaluation form (Figure 23) represents another approach and requires numerous other important pieces of information. The opportunity is described as a technical objective in conjunction with the products that meet this objective. Market size is an estimate from the developer's point of view and competitive products are descriptively outlined. Comments from the checklist results, the numerical evaluation, and the present status can be shown. Timetables that might be supplemented by CPM, PERT, or Gantt diagrams and charts are drawn for certain technical factors. The first quarter is divided into months, and the three successive quarters are not. When one is considering a venture opportunity, the fewer entries that appear in this section, the better the chance of rapid movement toward the market, because any anticipated delay due to technical development is lessened. Similarities with associated businesses and products is offered as justification for the business.

Figure 21. Needs–desires rating.

Criteria	Weight	X	Rating	=	Product
Needs (1)					
(2)					
(3)					
(4)					
(5)					
(6)					
Desires (7)					
(8)					
(9)					
(10)					
Total					

Figure 22. Probability-of-success chart.

Criteria	Weight	X	Rating	X	Confidence	=	Product
1							
2							
3							
4							
5							
6							
7							
8							
9							
10							
					Total		

The detailed product specification is critical. When this can be described, reproducibly met, and relied upon in the final products, business aspects will be more secure and can be more precisely defined. This is an obvious pivotal point on which the rest of the opportunity hinges. The final section on corporate impact can be used to list any statements showing how the technology will affect the company.

As for the use of models in the technical analysis, a model can be drawn and quantified. But experience with computer programs for technical analysis shows them to be too precise for the generally inaccurate and subjective assignment of input values. Innovative approaches to the modeling problem may result in improved analyses, but this is time consuming and often costly. It is better to avoid technical models and use the refined approach in marketing and financial areas. When such a method is desired, a body of appropriate literature on the subject is available for the technical developer to use before turning the opportunity over to the venture group.

Figure 23. Technical evaluation form.

Opportunity _____

Products _____

Estimated market size _____

Competitive products _____

Technical analysis, verbal evaluation _____

_____

_____

Technical analysis, numerical evaluation _____

_____

_____

Status _____

Time table

Task	Month	Month	Month	Quarter	Quarter	Quarter

Associated business and products _____

_____

_____

Product specifications _____

_____

_____

Corporate Impact
(Note: A full sheet is recommended for each topic.)

Technological implications

Market recognition

Social meaning

Competitive responses

Business cycle

Project investment to date

Engineering Analysis

In addition to the methods used for technical analysis, some separate methods can be applied to an engineering analysis. Before these are discussed, it should be pointed out that the distinction between engineering and technical analyses is arbitrary. The position taken here is that those items dealing with product background can be designated as technical detail, whereas product use and construction are engineering concerns. Manufacturing is a separate entity and basically deals with process, equipment, and production factors.

Engineering checklist. Two new evaluative techniques, one of them the checklist shown, would be specifically useful for engineering. It would deal with a separate set of criteria. There is no implication that it is representative or complete, but suggests some of the kinds of questions that might be asked. It can be followed in part or in its entirety to lay the groundwork for a numerical approach.

Checklist for Engineering Analysis

1. What is the status of product design?
2. Is design engineering required?
3. Is process engineering completed?
4. What kind of equipment is needed?
5. Where is special tooling required?
6. Does the capability exist internally?
7. Can the process be purchased externally?
8. Can the equipment be purchased externally?
9. Is maintenance or modification a major consideration?
10. Is the process familiar or unique?
11. What are the weak points?
12. Are there obvious expensive steps or equipment?
13. Can cost savings be developed?
14. Is the product structurally sound?
15. Are there better ways to make it?
16. Does it meet standards or regulations?
17. Can it be upgraded by modification?
18. Does it fit the existing product lines?
19. How does it compare to the competition?
20. What is the status of applications analysis?
21. What further applications research is required?
22. How is it to be packaged?
23. How is it to be shipped?

Chance of achievement. The second process in Figure 24 is a variation of the weighting-rating method. Here detailed scores are not required, and a general profile can be quickly developed. The criteria are listed and weighted according to the product or product line being evaluated. The chance of achieving the standards set by the criteria is then evaluated. If that achievement is an accomplished fact, the total-success column is checked. In that column, the definition of *total qualification* varies with each criterion, which differs from the other rating techniques described. If the process versatility is examined, for example, any process that is found substantially and recognizably better than existing operations for similar products might be rated as total achievement. If one is concerned with the company's current familiarity with the process, *total* might mean that it has been successfully demonstrated in a pilot plant. For structural properties, a rating better than that of any other product thus far encountered might be considered total achievement. Good ratings are those that show above-average performance. In the case of an innovation, no rating lower than that should be tolerated.

For venturing, a criteria rating below the average means that perhaps the product opportunity is not yet ready to be exploited. (This concerns only important criteria that require additional engineering effort.) The imaginative-imitation approach to new business marks an exception. Average scores are anticipated, with perhaps one or two outstanding engineering feats to justify the imaginative aspect.

Figure 24. Chance-of-achievement chart.

Criteria	Weight	Total (1)	Above Average (.75)	Average (.5)	Below Average (.25)	Reject (0)
(A)						
(B)						
(C)						
(D)						
(E)						
(F)						

In the final column, poor chance of achievement is headed *reject*. Ventures with factors that in themselves have a poor prospect are beyond a reasonable risk level. The purpose of analyses of this sort is to recognize shortcomings and the major contributions to high risk. New Venture Methodology is designed to limit risk in an already high-risk area, and only by eliminating or postponing those with inherently poor chances of success and achievement can this be accomplished.

Manufacturing Analysis

Manufacturing analysis consists of three segments, each of which contains numerous subsegments that frequently can be given dollar values. In each of the analyses described so far, little attention was given to the dollars-and-cents aspect. Not only can the manufacturing analysis be done with more ease because dollar definition is possible, but to do so is imperative. This does not mean that other rating techniques are inapplicable, only that cost analysis is an integral part if not the critical one.

The three segments of manufacturing analysis are the manufacturing process, equipment, and production. The process encompasses flow, utilities, people, automation, safety, job descriptions, and process descriptions. Equipment covers associated costs, rates of production, efficiencies, investment, and maintenance. Production uses input from the process and equipment functions, with all the additional factors relevant to the operation and the evaluation of production. Typical checklists to aid in production and manufacturing data collection are shown.

These checklists, however, do not yield data for the required economic job. The scheme in Figure 25 represents a model from which the economic aspects can be determined. The use of a computer program would be most helpful, but it must be designed to do the job according to individual needs. Each segment can be reduced to a systematic form to show how pertinent information is to be recorded.

Cost of goods. To determine costs of goods, direct and peripheral information is required. In Figure 25, each box represents a segment of necessary input. A process-flow diagram (box 1) that shows in detail the various steps and the materials balance is of great value. If it also describes isolated process phases, it will be helpful in future cost accounting. The flow diagram should designate the necessary equipment for the process with its ancillary parts and utility requirements. Raw materials at various stages of production, any additional process supplies, labor centers and space allocations, and other miscellaneous needs can be directly or indirectly developed from a refined process-

Production Checklist

1. Number, type, and quality of personnel
2. Job descriptions for classes of workers
3. Safety considerations
4. Process flow sheets
5. Automation and robotizing
6. Utilities; quantity, type, and usage rates
7. Itemized equipment lists
8. Equipment suppliers and service
9. Equipment rates, volume, capacity, efficiencies
10. Yields from process steps
11. Material balance
12. Building requirements
13. Site selection
14. Equipment salvage
15. Inventory levels, finished goods
16. Inventory levels, raw materials
17. Investment and depreciation
18. Expense budget, taxes, insurance
19. Cost accounting techniques
20. Working capital and accounts receivable

Manufacturing Data Collection

Raw materials
1. Are they currently available?
2. From whom?
3. Is the supply dependable?
4. Is the cost stable?
5. Are there special handling considerations?
6. Are they safe?
7. Are there special storage requirements?
8. Must the raw materials be preprocessed?
9. Are analyses and specifications available?

Products
1. Are they readily stored?
2. Are they sold by the present marketing organization?
3. Is the demand constant within limits?
4. Are there major price fluctuations?
5. Is there substantial competition?
6. Are they readily packaged?
7. Are there any shipping or transportation problems?
8. Is sales service extensively required?

Process
1. Is it unique in the industry?
2. Is it one of several alternatives?
3. Is it suited to present operational capabilities?
4. Is it technically developed?
5. Is it dependent upon key steps?
6. Are there special requirements?
7. Has waste disposal been solved?
8. Are there unusual materials of construction used?
9. Is it reliable and reproducible?
10. Are there any hazards?
11. Does it produce the desired product?
12. Are byproducts planned for?

flow diagram. The more accurately these can be defined in the analysis stage, the better the results will be. This assumes that equipment needs can be recognized by specific item and assigned a cost by a quotation or estimate from vendors. When the process definition is complete, the investment for the process equipment and installation (box 17) will be known, and the utility and subsequent raw material costs (box 3) can be calculated. When special utility requirements exist, it is best to be more precise than engineering estimates allow in order to get accurate utility costs (box 2). Raw materials (box 3) and process supplies (box 4) are based on the materials content of the fin-

Figure 25. Cost-of-goods flow.

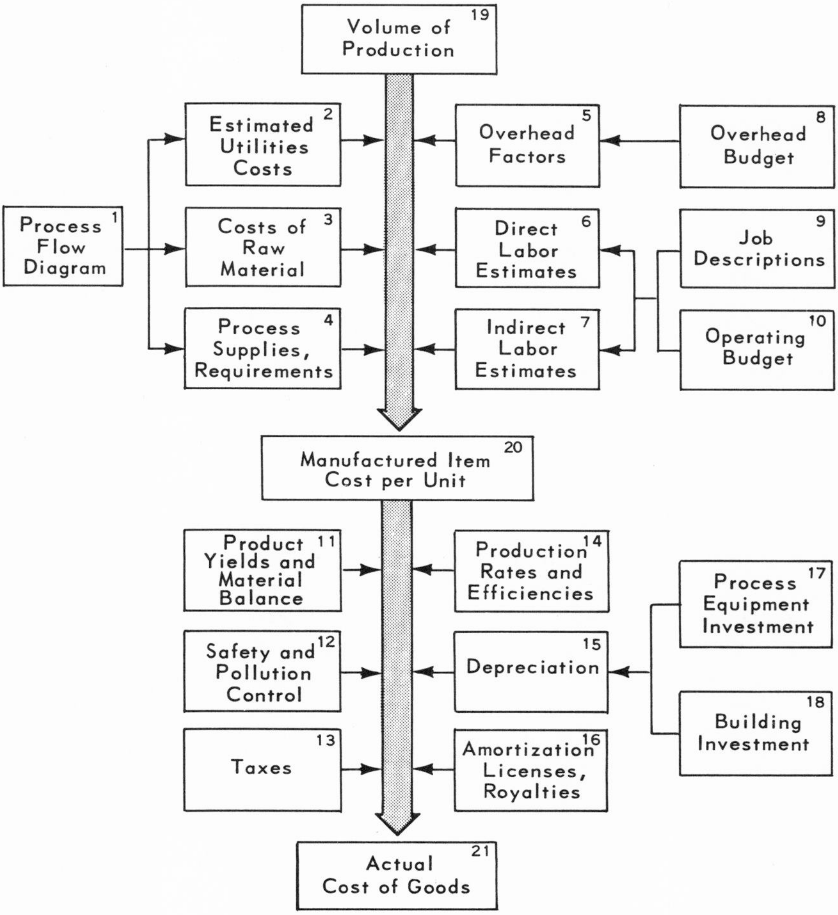

ished product. These theoretical figures are corrected in the second stage of the model by applying factors.

The overhead budget (box 8) can include some of the factors just discussed, but it also details many additional items. Typically, indirect labor elements are included in the overhead budget, but are shown separately here for clarity. Overhead items are included in a list with other first-order inputs, such as benefits, maintenance, property expenses, public relations and promotion, community relations, and many miscellaneous costs. Benefits include those supplements that the workforce has come to expect, like paid vacations and holidays, social security and hospitalization contribution, group life insurance, state disability insurance and workmen's compensation, overtime and shift premiums, pension, severance, and reclassification payments. Maintenance overhead that is not directly applicable to production would cover such expenses as machinery and equipment repair, including the cost of materials and replacement parts for manufacturing equipment; costs for relocation and rearrangement of everything from building partitions to office furniture; and maintenance of external items, including vehicles and materials-handling equipment, and upkeep of the building and grounds. Property expense would concern those costs associated with the land, buildings, personal property, and mobile items. Rental would be a major factor when the company does not own the property. This can be prorated on a space allocation basis, or can be directly determined from real estate or site-selection sources.

Two additional costs to consider are insurance on such things as the property, its contents, loss and liability, automotive and income protection, and business interruption coverage. Federal income taxes often account for an overwhelming share of the tax bite, but where real estate, personal property, and local operation licensing are concerned, more major costs could be encountered. Public and community relations and promotion (or in some cases local advertising) can be considered. These are not the same costs as those in marketing, but only concern the manufacturing center. For example, promotion might entail local literature mailouts revealing the company's social contributions and public awareness. Advertising might include want ads, agency fees, and participation in local functions. These could be defined as public or community relations, which might also include efforts like organizing local sports teams, holding open house, fund-drive cooperation, and setting up organizational memberships. Even though all of these expenses are anticipated, others may occur. The following list describes some of them.

Medical fees	Business, trade, and
Legal fees	professional memberships
Financial fees, audit,	Relocation expenses
tax, and consulting	Postage
Subscriptions	Travel
Meetings and conferences	Security
Contributions	Entertainment
Recruitment	Freight charges

Job descriptions (box 9), derived from the data on requirements, operations, and process stations, can be drawn up. These help to define the cost of direct labor when accompanied by a detailed study of local conditions. There are many texts to guide the form and content of the job descriptions. Demographics are available from many sources to make accurate estimates of labor rates for specific services. Jobs are generally categorized by salary range for skills at various experience levels. Wages can be related to national figures on given jobs, labor union contracts, or local conditions. Job descriptions with attendant proposed salary levels allow detailed derivation of the direct labor costs. The need for a process flow with appropriate designations for hourly workers is magnified by the fact that job descriptions, hence the direct labor costs, depend upon the accurate estimate of requirements for people in the process line.

The operating budget (box 10), which is somewhat simpler than the overhead budget, includes direct labor, material, supplies, and benefits. A typical one might show the direct labor costs by functional elements on a monthly basis. For example, a budget consisting of direct labor for eight process increments or subsegments indicates the number of workers required and the average wage range (Figure 26). Then a month-to-month cost is developed, finally describing a total figure for the year. This can be done for the first-year analysis or for several years of proposed operation. It is actually a planning document, which is then updated each quarter for the next twelve months. It describes changes due to expansion, automation, or other alterations. The same cost projection can be applied to indirect labor, listing each position with its estimated salary. The personnel in this case are all manufacturing people, directly chargeable to manufacturing costs. Administration and marketing would not be included in this analysis. This distinction can be difficult where one function is charged with multiple responsibilities. It is better to make unit differentiations than to assign parts of salaries to various categories.

The operating budget has other components not directly related to the manufacturing analysis that will be discussed later. It becomes

Figure 26. Direct labor budget.

	Average rate	Jan.	Feb.	Mar.	Apr.	May	June	July	Aug.	Sept.	Oct.	Nov.	Dec.	Total
Direct labor														
Press operators (4)	3.20													
Chemical operators (2)	3.15													
Mechanic (1)	4.10													
Cutter (1)	2.95													
Operators, general (3)	2.75													
Quality inspector (1)	3.65													
Packer (1)	2.75													
Addressographers (2)	2.50													
Total														

evident that the manufacturing analysis supplies data for the operating budget, and to some degree to the overhead budget, and that these data in turn are fed back into the financial analysis.

Finally, when volume of production is considered (box 19), the analyst selects estimates at several levels, typically a low or conservative figure, a high or optimistic figure, and a medium or most-likely one. The most-likely estimate should be used to develop the actual analysis, while the others supply final data to indicate the allowable degree of variance before major reorientations and new estimates must be made. Marketing analysis projections for yearly sales may also be an aspect of the total volume. It is reasonable to use a most-likely figure for a year when it is considered the venture will be operational or mature. However, it does not answer some of the financial questions concerning unit costs in preceding years. To determine this, a direct relationship between projected sales levels and manufacturing costs should be made. This may be preferred for financial purposes, but it is unrealistic from a business standpoint. Some losses can be anticipated during the very earliest business stages. Again, the emphasis is on the proper use of data derived from the manufacturing analysis. Achieving unit cost at an optimum sales rate is a venture objective. Recording unit costs of manufacture during commercial development stages makes the best guide for cash needs or dollar performance. Thus the low, high, and intermediate production levels are only helpful in mature stages, whereas the sales-related approach describes costs at various sales levels during business growth and development.

The cost per unit (box 20), described so far by the cost model, is based on standard rates of usage and costs for raw materials, supplies, utilities, and direct and indirect labor at chosen production levels. There are other considerations and variants that affect the actual cost of goods. These are handled separately for several reasons, the most important being that they are really related to the physical facility and operation of the business rather than the product. In some corporate situations these factors vary, often accounted for in separate cost-accounting centers or documents. For example, various taxes (box 13) are imposed on the facility. These can vary by state. A large corporation can deduct them, minimizing any venture losses, whereas a small business must accept the total incurred loss. Taxes for a venture housed within a corporation may be calculated on a full corporate base or some portion thereof, rather than on the venture as a separate company. The complexities of taxation are beyond the scope of this analysis, except to point out that specific assumptions should be made about those taxes not included in the overhead budget as guided by the financial arm of the company.

Another variable or set of unique costs includes the price of licenses, royalties, or the amortization of costs for technology or process rights (box 16). Where these are fixed by the number of unit items sold, the value can be readily calculated. If they are on sliding scales, absolute figures are more complex to develop and computerization of the model becomes a valuable asset. The method of payment of these commitments is usually set by a contract, and the amortization of these costs by company policy. Therefore they are dealt with on a variant cost basis, since they can change independently of the manufacturing process. Safety and pollution control (box 12) can be direct costs against manufacturing, but they are, in large or multiproduction centers, not always direct associated costs. Where an entire plant requires safety headgear, even office personnel are affected. The program cost may be shared or allocated or covered by a corporate allowance to meet these safety standards. As these examples indicate, the incorporation of cost elements must be tailored to the individual situation. It is important to include them, however, to be assured that the final cost of goods is as true a representation as can be made during the initial analysis and its subsequent updating.

The next three cost factors are also variable and require some background. The first concerns product yields and the basic materials balance within the process (box 11). (The materials balance is that amount of raw materials and supplies that can be directly related to the final product.) The methods for determining these are variants of those arising from the standard referred to in the process-flow and data descriptions. The variants are allowances that might be made for customer returns or breakage that would affect yields. Recycle credits can be incorporated to improve the materials balance. A number of factors deal with post-production product losses. They are specific for a given product and should be apparent to the analyst if he remembers to look for them. The materials balance can also be viewed in light of another approach that measures the stepwise conversion of materials into product and catalogs and evaluates the byproducts formed. Still another takes into account loss and wastage. The degree of productivity that falls outside specifications can be measured. As an adjunct to the latter, one can credit the value accrued due to the sale of seconds or out-of-specification material. Finally, one can recycle spills and broken, poor-quality, or returned goods. Cannibalization may be possible in cases of devices or built-up structures. All of these can be separated and fed back into the materials-balance calculation. Some are losses, others are credits.

Production rates and efficiencies (box 14) influence the actual cost of goods. This influence differs from that of volume of production, on which cost per unit is based. At lower levels of production, rates may not be adversely affected. This means that sufficient quantities of goods or material for sale can be produced in a relatively short period of time. The need for continuously employed staff can be replaced by part-time supervision, and some of the ongoing overhead may be alleviated. Some costs cannot be eliminated, but many can diminish. The result is lower unit costs, even at lower production levels. These efficiencies are but some of those possible. As the analyst views the manufacturing needs and the projected sales, other efficiencies might be discovered, and these are fed into the cost analysis.

Finally, consideration is given to depreciation (box 15) and allied costs, such as interest charges for invested capital, as they affect the actual cost of goods. This is not to say that interest and depreciation are interrelated elements, but it is convenient to combine them in this scheme. Depreciation can be handled several ways on fixed, or permanent, investment dollars. The land is not depreciated, but the structures will be. The building investment (box 18), if the factory is owned, or funds for improvement when facilities are rented, is depreciated according to a predetermined schedule. The rules for rate of depreciation that follow vary from a useful-life approach to the venture-life method. For tax purposes, several kinds of depreciation can be used. Straight-line depreciation for 20 years would pertain to the useful life approach, while a two- to five-year writeoff using double declining balance may be applicable for a short-term venture. These rules are usually set by corporate policy, or to best meet the requirements of an attractive tax position for an independent business. In evaluating the opportunity, one must be careful not to count too heavily on a tax advantage in early business stages. A longer-range view with confidence in the eventual success of the venture might yield better results. In any case, either a straight-line depreciation or an accelerated method can be chosen to best fit the circumstances.

The process equipment (box 17) is also depreciable at a choice of rates. The useful life, in conjunction with the venture or product life, should determine the rate. Either five or ten years on a straight-line depreciation to the salvage value of the equipment might serve best for analysis purposes. Any miscellaneous items, such as vehicles having specific depreciation problems, can be handled in the most appropriate manner or according to company policy. Other items, such as raw materials and finished-goods inventory, are not depreciable but do require capital that would not be available for other uses. This can be considered in the financial analysis through discounted cash methods, or interest on the encumbered capital can be charged against the produced goods. The same measures can be applied to the accounts receivable. These monies are tied up by customers' delays in payment for periods of time that depend upon the characteristics of the industry and the customer. If policy dictates, interest on these funds, at a rate arbitrarily chosen, can be charged against the venture through the product cost.

The final value assigned to the unit item is the actual cost of goods (box 21). The importance of this value is not to be underestimated. It not only demonstrates the high degree of process-engineering and manufacturing input, but serves as a base for the financial analysis, the market analysis, and the eventual pricing in marketing the product. It may seem that product has been overstressed here, and that to a service-oriented business, these items of cost do not apply. The same format does not fit, but the elements of cost should be reviewed and applied to the analysis by similar techniques tailored to the individual business. For small businesses or new independent ventures, these data can be as readily developed as they can in larger companies. Often the task is simpler, since cost factors are direct rather than indirect or applied. Profit relies upon the differential between income dollars from sales and expenses incurred, among which the manufacturing cost of goods is an important factor. Therefore, it is necessary to consider the manufacturing analysis as part of the critical triumvirate of manufacturing, marketing, and financial elements.

Market and Sales Analyses

It is not possible to present in this section the myriad vectors that influence the marketing of a product and the decision to market it. What will be discussed is the need to answer questions about predictions concerning the selling of the product or service. The single most-asked question in new business development is, "Will it sell?" The next is, "How much?" In order to justify expenditures, some indication of the dollars returning to the company through sales is required. Since so much depends on this estimate, marketing and sales potential must be made explicit. If the market dimensions are not stated, clearly delineated, and made a premise upon which decisions can be based, the elements of risk are disproportionately increased.

Recognizing the magnitude of this task, one must simplify the scheme used to analyze the data. New Venture Methodology recognizes the importance of a continuous supply of detailed information. Each aberrant piece of data weakens the projections to the point of jeopardy. Following is a discussion of the various factors used in developing the data, the types of critical data required, and the use analyses and presentation of that collection of facts and estimates.

But first, some definitions will help to direct the reader. The total-market figure for a product or service is often the most intangible of the quantities sought. Its vague nature derives from the proposition that any market grows as one broadens geographical boundaries, defines more miraculous properties, or sees lower and lower orders of end uses. The total market therefore represents a rather encompassing number that defines, through mathematical assumptions, the maximum sales figure that can possibly be obtained if every possible buyer purchased the product. A time orientation is generally applied, perhaps a fixed period such as a year. Because all purchasers are influenced differently and make various value judgments according to their individual needs, the total market will vary with the evaluator and the assumptions. Often there are limits placed upon the total market, which should be defined. If the emphasis is on the industrial market in the United States, then the concept of total market is accordingly restricted. If we begin to subjugate it further by using it to describe such things as present market, the original meaning loses all its impact. The total market, then, is the time-oriented, absolute, maximum quantity that could possibly be sold, within the broad parameters of user and geography. Present market, on the other hand, indicates the potential for growth and also shows the state of maturity of that product. In most cases the total market is not attainable, and only some portion of it is reasonably available. That portion is the potential market, a percentage of the total market that can be reached and has the capacity to purchase the goods or services. As most marketers are aware, pricing could eliminate some projected buyers. Volume, location, shipping charges, and numerous other factors eliminate some portion of the potential purchasers by design or chance. The remaining number is the value for the potential market. Again, the applicable time period should be specified. Complications enter the picture at this point since present market, when compared with the potential market, acquires a somewhat different meaning. Unless it is also segmented to match the assumptions used to develop the potential-market figure, it can be misleading and indicate a more difficult penetration problem. Penetration describes that portion of the potential market that can be captured in a given time period by the new entry. This is, of course, predicated upon two factors. The first is that neither the total nor potential market changes because of the introduction of a new technology. The second is that the offered product or service enhances the overall use pattern due to improvements in some segment of need or weakness. It is penetration that is used as the basis for sales projections, and is the single most complex appraisal to make. What happens when a totally new and innovative approach or product is concerned is another problem. Once such a distinction is made, a new conception of the market in all its ramifications has to be devised. Judgment in assessing the probable size of the new market is required, while it is still necessary to differentiate between the market in its broadest potentialities and the market within reasonable limits of potential achievement. When no product or service is presently available, a guessing game begins and techniques such as analogies can be employed. The rectitude of the estimates cannot be proved except in retrospect, but confidence in the capability of the entrepreneur or analyst and his sources must supersede emotional dimensions.

Developing the data. In most cases there is not a single, simple source of information. Once one locates relevant data, the need to corroborate it follows. It is easy enough to look for estimates in gross numbers, but all too frequently they emanate from some one source. It is not unusual to find specific market information through indicators or general product groupings that do not lend themselves to the customer or market segment of interest to the new venture. What it amounts to is that the best, most apt data commensurate with the product–market interaction is usually not available in a readily usable form. For this reason, a talented analyst must exploit all data sources and integrate them into a meaningful set of estimates that will suffice for the analytical phase. Such sources, similar to those described for sources of business opportunities, include the corporate market research team, the sales force, existing and potential customers and distributors, consultants, trade and government publications, and contacts. Government sources of demographics, used in conjunction with private information sources such as Predicasts and the Stanford Research Institute, are fruitful and comprehensive. The Bureau of the Census accumulates all manner of data besides counting heads. It conducts various annual surveys and keeps statistics on manufacturing by industry and locale. Industry reports on the production and shipments of commodities are also available from the Bureau. International trade can be surveyed through statistics compiled by the Bureau of International Commerce. Other bureaus, services, and special councils supply additional data that can be useful in many ways.

By using a comparative approach, one develops a cross check that increases one's level of confidence in the final market size values. The precise nature of chosen values is better in the short range than the long and should be accepted on this basis. Errors are magnified not only as projections proceed into the future, but when economics are developed on the basis of the market size in units or dollars. Other factors enter into interpreting data, such as the competitive situation, the present state and dynamics of technology, and the complexity of distribution to various consumer levels, including internal utilization. There are environmental factors that are not always apparent. The gathering of all available data is the primary objective. The second step is to select that which is critical to good forecasting.

Data for forecasting. The type of critical data required is similar to that used in typical sales forecasting. Here are some items that should be developed in depth. The total market should be segmented into individual product variations or services. By dividing the products into homogeneous groups, better resolution of the market is possible. Within this context, the further division into user categories will not only support the total-market data but will put greater focus on the relationships of pricing and perhaps distribution to the market analysis. A list of sales factors, including need, properties, pricing, and competition, can then be developed for the individual components. When these are laid side by side, the potential market, measured on a yearly basis, can be derived with a higher degree of certainty. The calculation is a combination of documented figures with judgment factors that can raise or lower the final estimates, depending upon the direction they indicate. The potential market is then defined numerically, and new product information is incorporated in the analysis. The initial positions taken and data presented in the technical and manufacturing analyses are utilized.

In conjunction with the other analysts on the venture, the marketing expert develops an initial penetration and a penetration rate. This becomes the first projected sales forecast for planning purposes. These are goal numbers based on the best estimates that the members of the venture team can produce. The approach used here is closely related to the executive opinion method of forecasting in which the best-informed executives join together to quickly obtain a sound figure. The difference here is the use of a systematic method rather than judgment. Sales-force data are invaluable, but where no sales force exists, no estimates are available. If market research has entered the picture in a supportive role, expectation of use or statistical projections can be supplied to guide and confirm the penetration calculations. This brings us to the plethora of other items needed for reasonable substantiation of the year-by-year planned projections for financial analysis.

Sales information. A price–volume curve indicates the possible sales volume at different consumer unit-cost levels. It is most difficult to define this for a multiline product or a multilevel distribution system. There are often different optimums of pricing among various market segments, and the degree of merchandising done in these segments would determine the sales volume. Delineating each segment by product, and planning how each portion would be serviced, are important parts of the analysis. Other income from selling ancillary items should be considered, and would be incorporated into the overall sales picture. These items might include smaller reorder units or perhaps a charge for service in case of special orders.

Sales expenses influence pricing and consequently sales volume. Delivery costs, which are sometimes absorbed in the price or are passed on to the customer in toto or as equalization rates allow, should be included in the sales determinations. If delivery costs are to be assumed by the seller, then the price of the products should reflect this. A cost–volume curve would be required to show what charges are reasonable from the customer's viewpoint and necessary for the effective and profitable operation of the business. The cost of packaging or crating not included in the manufacturing unit costs would also be taken into account. The payment of discounts or commissions in indirect selling efforts should be applied as a debit to the sales dollar projections.

In some cases, advertising is a major cost item. When a relatively high percentage of sales dollars is used for advertising and promotion, these costs need to be projected over the life of the venture. It is difficult to describe the expenditures in a linear projection since advertising is often campaigned. However, continuous incremental use of the media is advisable in some cases, and recognition of the approach to be used is valuable. Advertising costs during the first year, while introducing the product, are sometimes high. The second year they may be low as production struggles to keep up with the demand. As new markets or geographic areas are opened or as customers increase, funding is irregular and is coordinated to support this growth. The same kinds of information can be determined for technical service requirements. When problems occur they are frequently concentrated in one area of product performance because of some unforeseen occurrence. It is almost impossible to plan for this. When a continuous technical service budget is required, acknowledgment of this need is part of good market planning, and the appropriate dollar considerations should be made.

Test marketing, panels, field tests of various sorts, and activities related to direct selling are also considered part of sales costs. The complicated process of distribution, including warehousing, offices, vehicles, and other functions such as order control, invoicing, collections, accounting, and reporting, figures in the marketing scheme. The direct, fixed sales costs are, in themselves, a combination of many cost elements. The sales administration, salesmen, and service personnel account for salaries and expenses. When commissions are involved, additional factors are applied to the sales costs. Transportation, including investments in vehicles where applicable, can require a large dollar expenditure. Phone calls, postage, paperwork, and expense-account items can swell the budget and must be considered and controlled.

Finally, the array of literature that is often an integral part of product sales—technical literature, passouts, mail enclosures, specification sheets, salesmen's books, catalogs, logos, and other items—adds to the expenses that the marketing function must account for, and is properly included in the analysis. What it all adds up to is that a sales budget comparable to the detailed one developed for manufacturing is part of the analysis documentation.

Data utilization. The use of the data gathered in a comprehensive analysis that can be presented in a document reasonably well understood by readers from many disciplines is the subject of the following discussion. The data presumably have been collected and collated, to be supplemented by the analyst's judgment. The analyst has considered the many facets of the market and the merchandising of the product. The data are available and a format for the marketing analysis is needed. There is no one best or optimum way to present the marketing plan with its analysis. The plan, including approach and strategy, is inseparable from the economic evaluation. The "outline" in Figure 27 suggests a starting point. Its objectives are to define a dollar sequence for yearly sales for the business venture, and to structure the cost elements attributable to marketing. In each case the data are the only controls, and must be as vital and variable as the market and the venture's products. All pieces of data previously discussed can be developed independently from the detailed information and then joined to give a composite picture.

The total market is determined by gathering the information and then setting a value in terms of units and, hopefully, dollars. After certain assumptions and limitations are decided upon, a reasonable estimate of the potential opportunity will follow. This will be a percentage of the total market, and may or may not vary with time. For a computer program, a constant percentage for near-term is used, with allowances for increases as the time scale is expanded. The next step is to consider the factors on the left side of the illustration in Figure 27. Pricing, which is seldom considered in developing the total and potential markets, plays a role in defining the projected sales volume. It can be used to convert units to dollars, but more important is its effect on penetration volume. Figure 28 shows a typical curve marking the decrease in the volume of sales as the price in-

Figure 27. Projected sales volume input.

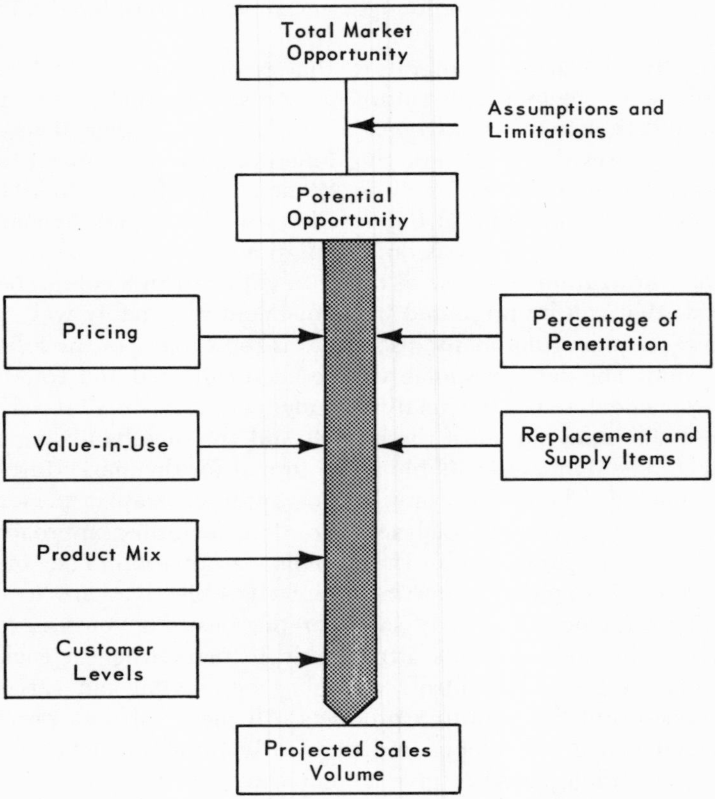

Figure 28. Volume price curve.

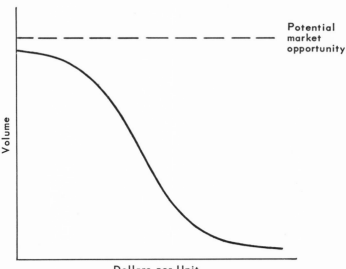

creases. The price sensitivity described by this curve is extreme, although in many instances of new products in which need predominates, it may not hold. It also may turn out to be a go, no-go situation, in which no volume is anticipated above a certain price. It is possible for volume to show such a cutoff with unit price, as is a stepwise change in volume, rather than describing a smooth curve as shown.

The second consideration is value-in-use, defined here as the total cost to the user of the product in its final functional form. This includes any components of the end use that are not integral to the initial product and that are required to put it in the proper state to serve its final intended purpose. Examples of these components would include such things as installation, safety covers, and ancillary attachments where the initial product is the major component. Where the product is a minor component of a large device, such as the plug on an electrical appliance, other factors control its more limited value-in-use. Where the part is critical and is not easily replaced, the value-in-use increases. The judgment must be made according to each case.

Once the value-in-use range is determined and price is considered a constant, a curve such as that shown in Figure 29 can be developed. As value-in-use increases, the volume of units that can be sold

Figure 29. Value-in-use curve.

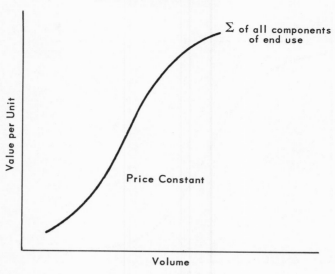

Volume

at the stated price increases. This is also a factor in the calculation of projected sales volume. Similar deliberation on the character of the product mix is required. Where a single product is concerned, this is not applicable. When variations on the same product result in different manufacturing considerations, marketing approaches, or pricing, elaboration of the mix is necessary.

Figure 30 presents one form of a table to describe the various

Figure 30. Dollar sales by product.

	Year				
	1	2	3	4	5
Product A	100	200	300	300	300
Product B	20	60	90	120	150
Product C	– –	10	15	20	25
Product D	75	65	55	45	40
Product E	5	5	15	20	25
Total Mix	200	340	475	505	540

Figure 31. Customer levels.

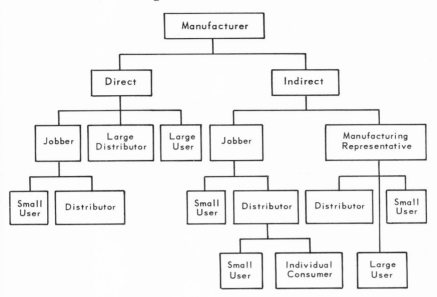

products involved. The importance of this breakdown is that it identifies the items that will contribute to growth and the point at which they will evolve in the time sequence. In some instances, Product A could be Market A, and so on, which in turn could represent the geographic area, type of customer, or some other specific aspect of the business being analyzed. A hypothetical flow of product to user is shown in Figure 31. Not only does the description help in developing a market plan, but it shows how pricing can escalate through the distributional chain. It also clarifies how internal competition might occur and helps to map strategy. It further helps the analyst avoid making the assumption that the sales price set by the manufacturer does not grossly affect the ultimate user's view of value-in-use when levels of distribution are involved. Within this series of interrelated distributional factors, the percentage of penetration by each can be calculated. When the model is adapted to a computer program, one of the outputs is the amount following each path. When other ancillary items of sale accompany or follow the initial sale, they can be added separately or carried as part of the product mix. Paper for a copying machine would be an example of a situation in which sales are related directly to the number of machines in use. The results of this exercise are the projected sales volume on a yearly basis for the prescribed length of time for justification of the venture, and a properly detailed and informative analysis.

Cost summary. The last segment of the mathematical analysis of marketing is outlined in Figure 32. This is the manifestation of the cost elements detailed previously. The commissions and discounts entry warrants some comment. In some accounting procedures for planning, these items are directly applied against the projected sales volume. This is possible when the forecast has been converted from units to dollars, to give actual income figures rather than to use artificial numbers with paper charges against the income. With commissions, the allocation of these dollars as a marketing expense is more

Figure 32. Cost as applied to goods.

	Years		
	1	2	3
Manufacturing costs			
Direct sales expenses			
Commissions and discounts			
Distribution expenses			
Packaging			
Advertising and promotion			
Administration costs			
Facilities			
Equipment			
Paperwork			
Technical Service			
Market Development			
Subtotal: Costs as Applied to Goods			

appropriate and can be handled accordingly. After all these elements are determined and added to the manufacturing costs, a total is reached that describes the applied costs. The research or miscellaneous service charges such as legal assistance, taxes, and others would also be included. Combining these yields the margin between sales income and the cost of doing business. In this manner, New Venture Methodology, through careful and complete analyses, describes the worth of the venture opportunity to the company's growth and profits.

Financial Analysis

Of course, both the manufacturing and market analyses are financial in character. The aspect of concern here is that of the relative profitability of various investment opportunities and their (potential) absolute fiscal contribution to the company in terms of conventional and modern economics. Because no one method is conclusive, several will be discussed. The complete and detailed ramifications of all the financial yardsticks cannot be handled within this text, but the alternatives that can be employed are recognized and presented.

Return on investment. The first and most popularly referred to yardstick is return on investment. The various ways of calculating this vary from simply placing after-tax profits in the numerator of the fraction and total investment in gross assets in the denominator, to rather complex equations. Progressive refinement of the simplest form leads to a number of possible alternatives. ROI can be calculated before taxes so that the venture does not have to carry the burden of the high tax rate that applies to the composite corporation. This technique may better describe the venture as an independent entity without necessarily neglecting the after-tax returns at the corporate tax rate. Smaller businesses may not need both figures, though their calculation is straightforward and does not require an expanded information base.

Another refinement is cumulative profit and investment over a period of years, which determines the yearly average by dividing the final figure by the number of years. One can also depreciate the fixed investment and use a diminishing investment number. The present value of the investment is applicable in cases in which the investment is written off on a longer term than the life of the venture. If the venture continues beyond the depreciation period, the investment theoretically diminishes to zero and the ROI approaches infinity and becomes meaningless. When working capital is included in ROI, the calculation does not become academic, but it does have a different meaning and should be redefined as return on total capital. The discounting of cash income and inflation of the investment with time can be incorporated in the formula to yield a truer cash value for the numerator and denominator over the time span of the venture. This kind of manipulation has advantages in that it clarifies the actual dollar worth as well as ROI, but it can become too complicated for effective communication.

Another method that has been described in the literature is the development of the various components of cash flow, resulting in such designations as turnover and return on sales. The formulas follow several steps that separate the relationship of sales to expenses from that of sales to investment.

Sales − cost of sales = earnings

Working capital + fixed investment = total investment

$$\frac{\text{Earnings}}{\text{Sales income}} = \text{return on sales}$$

$$\frac{\text{Sales income}}{\text{Total investment}} = \text{turnover}$$

Return on investment = return on sales × turnover

Previously ROI was described as the before-tax earnings divided by total investment. This reiterates the primary, simple approach, but it is related to other yardsticks valuable in planning and then monitoring a business. Cost of sales would necessarily include manufacturing, technical, marketing, and administrative expenses. Depreciation would not be involved, nor would discounting be applied. The working capital would be composed of funds for inventory, accounts receivable minus accounts payable, short-term debts, and cash on hand. Return on sales is utilized in low-investment businesses, and turnover is helpful in high-investment businesses. By using a formula such as that shown above, all of the factors can be examined as they are incorporated, and the various relationships can be judged. The converse is also true, since ROI, once determined, can be supported by a review of the important elements.

ROI can serve as a means of assuring and controlling the proper implementation and attainment of goals put forth in plans and objectives. It becomes part of the general fiscal plan that includes various performance reports. The control factors that result when the venture matures also show a measure of the success of the venture. During commercial development, the evaluation of the plans, the analysis of variants, and the identification of cost centers all point to the profit plan and to the measures required to reach the planned plateaus. In no case will the financial tools substitute for individual judgment. But their simple and flexible use allows decision making based upon data that are easily communicated and mutually understood.

Cash flow. Another evaluation in the process is the cash-flow analysis. The total investment figured as the sum of all fixed and working investment increments over the period measured (in the case of ventures, those are the investments anticipated) represents the cash required. Cash is generated by sales income minus those expenses incurred in developing and maintaining the business. Cash generated is then used to offset cash needs. The difference between them is the cash flow. It is a negative migration during the early years when income is limited, and it becomes positive as sales grow and the venture moves into commercial development and maturity. The benefit of the cash-flow figures is that appropriations can be planned and the desired change from outflow to income can be determined. This calculation can be handled simply, or it can include credits for depreciation included as a manufacturing debit, credit for tax savings during loss periods as it is affected in a larger corporation, and discounts for the time value of money. If the same dollars are invested in a going business or in some known-return securities, the earnings can be predicted. Another factor to consider is that inflation has been eroding the value of the dollar. When these are integrated into the cash flow, a discounted cash flow can be developed. The dimensions of the evaluation depend upon the compound factor or factors used. Computer programs are available that carry out this exercise and are flexible enough to handle the many variations.

With the cash-flow curve, a break-even point becomes obvious. This is a point in time at which the figure for cash generated is a positive number. The investment is, of course, tied up for the life of the venture, but the equivalents in dollars are paid back from the profits generated. This payout is an accounting description of the recovery of the initial cash investment, occurring where the cumulative net cash flow passes the zero line on a continuous graph. This should not be confused with the break-even that describes the zero profit point in a venture, which is also effectively used for comparison or demonstration. In ventures, the basic idea is to tie up a minimum amount of cash during the early stages of market development. By carefully analyzing the flow, an appropriate time-oriented allocation of investment can be made to minimize the risk.

The useful life of the venture can be projected as part of these calculations, and this would affect several of the determinants. There are
many reasons for cessation of a venture, which are considered in the
section on maturation. At any given time, some residual value is necessarily attributable to the venture. Rather than attempt to predict an
end point, the venture leader measures residual value continuously in
terms of assets of a going business within another organization. This
allows one to choose an appropriate time to sell the assets and good-
will for a maximum generation of cash, if this is the choice. The value
can be simply identified as a selected factor, multiplied times the
sales volume, plus fixed assets, inventory, and know-how. Another
means of evaluating the business is to apply the present worth factor
using several interest or discount rates. The advantage of this method
is that the inherent value of the business will be growing with time
and can help offset apparent small returns in large sales operations
with large investment. To arrive at present worth, present value is
added to the difference between cumulative income and cumulative expenditures, and then the residual value is added as described
above.

Other financial documents can be used as part of the analysis.
Many of these will become reporting vehicles after the risk group
moves into commercial development. The description here, however, is
limited to those that will clarify the analysis and support venture
planning. These are shown in Figures 33–37.

Consolidated income statement. The modified income statement
that appears in Figure 33 is an overview or summary of the income
and expense elements resulting in operating income to the company.
Several aspects of the income statement are helpful in the financial
analysis phase. Revenues from sales have to be projected as accurately as possible. This yields the growth curve and then growth rate
can be calculated. Where income is derived from sources other than
the main product or service objective, it would be included under
revenues and labeled as to its specific source. Costs and expenses,
determined in the marketing and manufacturing analyses, are described by general expense titles, showing where money is spent in
support of sales. The pretax income from which ROI can be calculated is the difference between revenue and the costs and expenses.
Taxes are estimated, or where they are defined by the venture, they
are arithmetically derived and subtracted from pretax income to
yield the net income. When investment is shown, the ROI for each
year can be quickly evaluated. Using this format, the rate of investment build-up also becomes evident. The return on sales is also

shown to assist in reaching some conclusions concerning the progress of the projected commercial development.

Operating budget. The operating budget figured on a month-by-month basis can take a form like that shown in Figure 34. The particular cost centers corresponding to those described in previous paragraphs force some in-depth thinking about the character of the venture operation. To carry it for five years would be arduous and somewhat unrealistic. If a proposal requiring two or perhaps three years were presented in support of the other documentation, a strong case for cash requirements could be made. Some of the headings represent sums of smaller expenditure items and can be handled on separate documents if required. This budget does not show income or margins, though it is based on production rates and sales efforts to meet the projected sales shown in the other forms. The totals show the areas of expense in relation to each other. The monthly sums show a

Figure 33. Consolidated income statement.

	Year				
	1	2	3	4	5
Revenues Net sales					
Costs and expenses					
Pretax income					
Taxes					
Net income					
Investment					
ROI					
ROS					

Figure 34. Operating budget.

| Expense category | Month | | | | | | | | | | | | |
---	Jan.	Feb.	Mar.	Apr.	May	June	July	Aug.	Sept.	Oct.	Nov.	Dec.	Total
Manufacturing													
Direct labor													
Indirect labor													
Direct materials													
Benefits													
Supplies													
Utilities													
Travel													
Sales													
Direct labor													
Advertising													
Promotion													
Administration													
Total													

Figure 35. Inventory and working capital requirements.

Inventory	Jan.	Feb.	Mar.	Apr.	May	June	July	Aug.	Sept.	Oct.	Nov.	Dec.	Total
Raw materials													
Standard													
Components													
Standard													
Partial products													
Standard													
Finished goods													
Standard													

Working Capital	Jan.	Feb.	Mar.	Apr.	May	June	July	Aug.	Sept.	Oct.	Nov.	Dec.	Total
Total inventory													
Standard													
Accounts receivable													
Standard													
Accounts payable													
Standard													
Cash													

picture of reasonable variation, continuous growth, or unusual monthly requirements.

Inventory. Figure 35 shows two items, but they are not necessarily handled, under practical situations, as one unit. Inventory is a component of working capital, and it is convenient to place the working capital analysis in close proximity to the inventory analysis. These are also month-to-month reckonings, and might be charted for a two-year period. Beyond this, monthly detail is specious and yearly estimates suffice. A standard can be used if it is developed beforehand. This allows a programmed need for inventory dollars, and individual entries show only the deviation or variance from the standard. Working capital, described in the lower chart, uses the same approach. Cash, however, does not follow the pattern since the standard is zero and all needs are deviations. Accounts payable are entered as negatives and put in parentheses, subtracting from inventory those amounts for items that are held by the company but not paid for as of the date of entry. Just as customers are sometimes delinquent in making payment, the company or venture might be delayed in paying its vendors.

Figure 36. Investments.

	Value	Depreciation rate	Dollars of depreciation
Permanent Land			
Buildings			
Equipment			
Goodwill			
Patents			
Licenses			
Working capital Inventory			
Accounts receivable			
Cash			
Prepaid expenses			

Figure 37. Business venture economics.

	Year							
	1	2	3	4	5	6	7	Total
Opportunity Potential Penetration Sales projections Other income								
Direct labor Indirect labor Benefits Direct materials Miscellaneous items								
Depreciation Amoritization Property costs								
Sales costs Discounts or commissions Advertisement and promotion Distribution								
R&D Miscellaneous								
Subtotal								
Investment margin								
ROI								

Investments. The investments shown in Figure 36 are permanent or fixed investments, which would be entered on a separate sheet for each year surveyed in the analysis. This serves multiple purposes. It gives definition to the future need for new investment and other cash flows for growth, distinguishes between the various types of expenditures, and gives overall recognition for spending corporate or venture funds, upon which many monitoring factors depend. This chart also can reflect the assignment of depreciation rates and calculate the actual dollars attributable to depreciation. Working capital is duplicated on this chart, but in absolute terms only, not as a variance from a standard. Where no depreciation is applied to an investment, as occurs with land and working capital, the space would be left blank on the chart.

Business venture economics. The business venture economics chart in Figure 37 is a planning and reporting form that conveniently summarizes some of the tasks the preceding forms are designed to analyze in detail. As the data are developed and projected for several years (five years being considered reasonable, ten difficult, and some in-between number of years for reaching payout or break-even regarded as acceptable), a single source of the economic conclusions becomes very valuable. The duplication of information is readily apparent, and again, the income from projected sales is shown in relation to the opportunity and the potential. Penetration is a percentage of the potential, giving the projected sales figure. Expenses for manufacturing, depreciation, sales costs, research, and miscellaneous items, when subtracted from income, leave a margin. When investment is shown, and an ROI calculated, a ready reference for planning and proposal purposes is available.

The financial analysis can be as detailed or as complex an accounting approach as is desired by the analyst, the decision maker, or the corporate body. The charts shown here are easily used by the various venture people who will be living with the venture and by those to whom the proposal is directed. These charts are pragmatic approaches and may fall short of the long-range need. Such operating documents and accounting procedures as are necessary for operation must be put into use as soon as the analysis phase is preempted by venture development.

Legal Analysis

In-depth legal advice is best sought from an attorney who has expertise in the fields in question. The role of the analyst in preparing a legal analysis is to recognize problem areas, obtain the documentation, get the necessary advice for guidance, and define the areas where professional services will be required. Legal questions must be satisfactorily addressed prior to the venture development phase. It is not the judgment of the analyst that prevails in this case but that of the legal counsel. Broad areas of consideration can be discussed in the context of the need for professional services where a potential problem exists.

Patents. The first of these areas might be the patent search. It should be made by the analyst using likely sources such as abstracts and the *Patent Gazette.* It is important to know what the present state of the art is in terms of practice and of earlier, perhaps still-unused, disclosure. The life of the patents, who holds them, the status of coverage for the venture, and peripheral disclosures that might be damaging are a few factors to be integrated in the analysis. The relative importance of patents to the decision maker should be understood so that the degree of definition required is known. Patents can be ordered and read, and the references cited should be researched. It is important to know the patent positions in the countries in which submissions are to be made, both in the case of new patents or of patent positions already established, not only for international ventures but for domestic ones as well. Growth may engender moves overseas that might suddenly be barred by some unforeseen patent problem. Where proprietary knowledge is involved and patent coverage is not likely, other legal protective measures might be suggested.

Licenses. The matter of licenses is linked with that of royalties. In both cases, agreements and contracts are integral parts of the analysis. The payment of royalties that might accrue as a result of agreed utilization of someone else's patents or know-how would need detailed explanation, and at least preliminary data on mutual intent, before further action could or would proceed. There are other factors that might be considered in this segment of the analysis. The role of codes and regulations, both local and federal, should be evaluated. Where food products and drugs are concerned, some rather detailed and comprehensive analysis must be made in conjunction with the governing agency and the source of technical support. The best way to do this is to draw up a checklist tailored to the company, its attitudes about the legal aspects, the type of business concerned, and the technological status of the industry or field.

Finally, the analyst will recognize the need for legal backup in cases of joint ventures, in the purchase of technology, in acquisition, and in hiring an entrepreneur along with his business opportunity or development. It does not pay to get bogged down in legal entanglements at the beginning of the venture, or to overemphasize this portion in the overall analysis. It is imperative to secure written advice and opinions on difficult questions or issues that could result in rejection of the venture as a nonviable opportunity for the company.

Venture Analysis

While this term is not strictly a financial concept, it refers to the application of dollar quantification to the overall venture aspects. It is gaining increasing relevance at management levels for decision making, where it is used for evaluating new business opportunities.

The factors involved in venture analysis are similar to those in the preceding analyses. Although specific meanings have been attributed to the term *venture analysis,* it has come to mean a technique for judging and comparing new projects at multiple levels of management on the basis of various inputs from mathematical evaluations of the product, process, and market. By implication, it entails a rather sophisticated set of methods, handled by computer applications, for assistance in making decisions. In each instance, its major function is modeling the technical, engineering, marketing, production, and financial factors into a systematic approach.

Most information concerning the new business opportunity comes in small discrete parts. These pieces must be coordinated into a recognizable format in which each part helps to clarify the others. Venture analysis keys this knowledge through appropriate quantification into a financial scheme. In addition to the analyses discussed, one should take into account a few unique considerations. Because each consideration increases complexity, the manual approach to quantification is replaced by the mechanistic. Computer programs, whether standard or internally generated for a specific company (seldom for a single venture), must be used to handle complex calculations. The heart of the procedure is proper modeling. This is the clever and logical use of technical, engineering, manufacturing, market, and sales information. The subordinate factors in these categories have been detailed in previous paragraphs. Added to the obvious aspects of business analysis, explicit consideration of other factors in the market can be identified. The effect of competition, timing, obsolescence, and internal product replacement are better understood and considered. These are the first of the uncertainties to be applied to market penetration in terms of dollar sales. Other uncertainties occur within all the parts of the basic analyses. These were alluded to in several of the documents recommended for use by the analyst. The next sequence would formalize these uncertainties through familiar computer tools. Profiles of uncertainty would make the decision maker aware of the chance or likelihood of a certain outcome. Risk analysis would then include uncertainties in the performance values and tables, showing the probability of achieving or missing the anticipated results. One can use confidence curves with certain probability limits, Monte Carlo sampling, and game theory to reach the decision based on various broad bands of risk. One can apply these to the analyst's original data with superimposed variables when doubts or questions remain. Formal decision analysis can be applied to the simulated venture. Alternatives can be compared, and answers to the problems that might arise can be supplied and the outcome evaluated, according to the solution applied. Again, this is a tool for the decision maker, and it is only as good as his ultimate judgment and the input.

All these tools in venture analysis require skill to use, time to develop, and desire to implement. Management must be committed to understand, accept, and utilize them. The greatest insight is needed to decide where the limited investment funds of the company will go. To augment these intuitions, the judgment of the analyst, and the descriptions of the various analytical forms, venture analysis can help bring in improved future revenues from the expended funds. In March 1961, S. L. Anderson described venture analysis as

> . . . a technique of economic planning for the commercialization of new products, concerned with guiding decisions in the early stages of planning. There are four characteristics of the problem of commercializing research which are troublesome to the manager, troublesome in the sense that they engender a desire to delay decisions until a firmer basis can be developed for choosing among the many alternatives available to him. These four characteristics are:
>
> 1. Complexity of market, and investment and cost factors influencing profitability of venture.
> 2. Multitude of alternatives to be evaluated quantitatively before selecting a course of action.
> 3. Risk introduced by forecast uncertainties.
> 4. Possible counteractions by customers and competitors.
>
> Venture analysis is a method of analyzing alternate strategies of commercializing new products or processes which permits more explicit consideration of the risks introduced by the forecast uncertainties and the potential counteraction of customers and competitors who must adjust their tactics in the face of a new factor in the market. This type of analysis relies heavily on large-scale digital simulation of the entire business enterprise. The primary purpose of the analysis is to reduce the desire to delay decisions by being appreciably more quantitative in foreseeing the economic consequences of alternate commercialization routes under a variety of circumstances.
>
> Some of the decisions taken into consideration have been: pricing policy, degree of product differentiation, plant capacity, forward integration, and number of end-use markets to develop.
>
> Some of the uncertainties which have been taken into account to evaluate risk have been: size of markets, rate of market penetration, degree of product substitutability, investment and cost assumptions, and duration of military markets.

6

The Product

In the discussions of the various analyses, characteristics of the product were included as necessary considerations. This section will not only. reflect upon product characteristics but product properties, product–market relationships and the manufacture of the product. The nature of the product requires evaluation because it plays a role in determining pertinent facets of product planning. The assumption is so often made that the product is new or unique, resulting in difficulty in preparing specific engineering and market justification to support the venture premise. More frequently, the product is not entirely new, but is an innovation to the company and to its marketing organization. When it is truly new to the market, the preparation and planning do require more insight and effort. The commodity under consideration for a venture might be a service. In that case, only certain portions of this chapter would be applicable. Since, however, services are so often associated with products, this chapter would be worth exploring. Perhaps the best place to start is with the evolution of a new product.

Product Characteristics

Product Evolution

The first awareness of an opportunity for a new product might arise from an obvious market need or a technical capability developed internally or externally. Considering it a need implies that the

114

consumer knows what he wants. In many cases this does not hold true. The need is more frequently apparent to a casual though perhaps imaginative observer because it has been downgraded, ignored, or buried in a maze of other problems by the using agency. As a means is developed or located and defined to control, adapt, reorient, or solve the problem caused by the need, the criticality of the problem is brought to the fore and it is given appropriate attention. It is important to know what the consumer wants, but his need may be something he is not yet aware of or has learned to do without. For this reason an imaginative approach is required, with an eye to finding a possible means for filling the need.

The technical capability should be developed coincidentally with the recognition of need. However, the means is seldom coincidental to the market or developed to fit its needs. There are exceptions, but more frequently, predetermined and demonstrated technology is available, awaiting modification and innovation to mesh with the market need and resulting in a business opportunity. If the means is in hand, the clever merchandizer ferrets out the need and boldly informs the potential customer that he now has a solution to the latter's often hidden problem. There have been many discussions in the literature on new-product development about market needs and technological capability. In venturing, the critical point is to find an opportunity in which these two are combined. An aggressive, imaginative approach makes an important contribution to the effort to convince the marketplace that a task can be done better, more economically and efficiently, and more quickly by the venture group's product. So product evolution is not a cut-and-dried matter, but a series of continuous and responsive activities that result in a product for a specific market.

If evolution could be idealized, it might be represented by a coherent spiral from inception to final product. As previously outlined, the four I's are idea, invention, innovation, and improvement. Added to these, imaginative imitation provides a source of business opportunity. Wherever the product starts from the venture standpoint, it must have originated as an idea. The idea grows out of knowledge and cumulative learning combined with the experience of one or many people, all ultimately integrated into a coherent package by an individual. Once the idea is presented, it can then be put into practice through some type of trial or experimentation. This part of the evolution becomes repetitive and cyclic as improvements become apparent and modifications are incorporated. The technical development is reviewed at some stage in terms of the possible end use.

The next step is the process development for reproducibly manu-facturing the product. Market development follows, with appropriate attention to consumer response, in-use performance, and necessary modification and improvement. A product description can then be settled upon according to the specifications and standards estab-lished. Distribution is designed and sales strategy is implemented, re-sulting in actual market use of the product. Feedback from the mar-ketplace induces further innovation and subsequent product extension and expansion. The sequence is seldom ideal, and there is frequent retrenchment and reevaluation throughout.

Just where New Venture Methodology operates in the product evolution is not easily indicated. Much depends upon the venture objectives and charter. Assuming that ideas and inventions are too premature for venture consideration, we would choose the stage of product evolution sometime after its reduction to practice for a start-ing point. If we accept this assumption with its strong arguments and justifications, the discussion of product characteristics can be con-sidered with a specific product in mind. From this point of departure, the attributes are analyzed.

Attribute Analysis

A formal document can easily be developed to describe the char-acteristics of the product aside from the technical, manufacturing, and marketing aspects. The product, at the prototype stage of devel-opment, can be defined by its physical properties, but the tendency to catalog and emphasize the wrong or the least important ones presents a very great problem. Because it is time-consuming to include extra-neous tests for minor properties, the need to make a careful selection of the appropriate major attributes cannot be overstated. Some physi-cal properties might seem appealing superficially, but have no rela-tion to the intent of the market or the need of the customer. The dis-tinction between need and desires will be touched upon later in this discussion. Mechanical properties may be more critical in some prod-uct areas than others. These would, of course, be related to end use, and characterization should be directed that way. Specific properties describing the engineering qualities would not only be of interest to the user but could define potential product limitations to the analyst. In addition, some estimate of the need for research support to test, evaluate, or improve the properties in terms of manpower, time, and money would be made. In the same vein, mention of a knowledge of the servicing requirements to support market development and commercialization should be included in the attribute study.

Product description. It should go without saying, but it is ignored so frequently, that there is need for an exact, detailed product description. It could be a mere one-sentence statement, but it should be sufficiently comprehensive and include all critical aspects. The product description that can be continuously updated keeps everyone who is involved informed about this portion of the venture direction. Product definition and specification may remain loose until more knowledge and experience are fed into the system. The product description provides a constraint so that the course of the venture is not diverted by arbitrary modifications in specifications. Another component of the description is the structure and content of the product line. When a mix of products is inherent in the venture, some indication of the relative portions of the business each will capture is imperative. Definition of the individual portions helps to better describe the business and the requirements for supporting it. It also allows for some prognostication concerning growth and extensions of the product line, both in the near and longer-range future. It may seem premature to be concerned about additions to the product line at this point, but the venture may rely on such planning for continued growth at the projected rates set by corporate objectives.

Application analysis. Two subanalyses of the attribute analysis would be an application analysis and a value-in-use study. The application of the product, especially when it is a component of another product, is as important as the product properties. Stating it often helps refine the delineation of properties and reinforces projections and estimates of needs. It is necessary to be specific. Its inclusion directly in the analysis generally relies upon market data dealing with the final product. One cannot be haphazard about assessing the final product market, yet a secondary product study is not justified. The data developed do help in the areas of labor input and installation, steps in the use of the venture product that were not apparent in the original product. This information goes hand in hand with the value-in-use consideration. Value-in-use in this case represents the integration of all cost elements, plus the estimated value of intangibles to the consumer in his utilization of the product. The costs of some of the elements are obvious. For example, existing products may need further work prior to use, while the new product of the venture can be used without further effort. This increases its value-in-use. Work expended on present products may include parts, materials, labor, and investment, any of which could be eliminated in the new product.

Other costs—installation, for example—will be discovered in the study of value-in-use. There are items to which no actual out-of-pocket funds can be assigned. Some attempt at fixing dollar values for these might be made, or they can follow as verbal addenda to the product-value section. Convenience, service, returns, replacements, fast shipment, precision, and other desirable features can be included in value-in-use. For example, a lower return rate does save time and postage as well as telephone calls, excuses, frustration, and slowdowns. What are these worth? Judgment is again important, and serves to quantify the value. As a note of caution, the value-in-use figure should not be based on overly sophisticated or complicated formulas. It is only worthwhile if it is easily understood and accepted and has some universality in its meaning. The common elements can be included, but any suspected of being specious cast doubt on the whole concept. A job well done in this area becomes an excellent tool for marketing.

In general, an attribute analysis should include:

Product description
Product specifications
Product line
Product extension
Application analysis
Value added
Value-in-use

The first portion corresponds to the preceding discussion on the product description, product line, or product mix. The potential growth areas are designated product extension. A chart on properties, individualized for the product in question, would comprise an important segment of the analysis. The application analysis, value added, and value-in-use can be incorporated following the description of product characteristics, each adhering to the preceding discussion. In the case of value added, a concept that was covered in detail, the information first supplied is the position of the product in the chain of usage from raw material to ultimate use. Adding the contribution made by the company in transforming starting materials to a salable form helps to reveal the potential of future forward or backward integration. All these segments of analysis thoughtfully prepared will help the analyst and serve as supporting documentation for a business proposal.

The Product and the Market

Comparatives

Two types of comparative listings are pertinent in examination of the product. One is the cataloging of desirable features (advantages) and the undesirable ones (disadvantages). These can be used by themselves or in conjunction with similar lists for competitive products. Another is the delineation of product requirements, which have a different degree of importance than the options. A cautious approach circumvents the desirable properties and concentrates on the mandatory ones. It can be painful to watch a product fail in the marketplace because of improper emphasis on its desirable features rather than on those critical to acceptance and performance. It might also be of value to use the advantages and disadvantages of the venture product, and of competitive ones, for numerical ratings and evaluations. The relative scores can at least show the gross degree of innovation offered by the venture product. The requirements are the criteria used in this analysis phase and can be condensed for clarity in the product outline.

Product Type

When the relationship of the type of product to the company's capabilities and to the market is reiterated, four types of product entries are disclosed. The first is that when introduction of a new model or an improvement of a present product is contemplated. This is relegated to the operational division's effort. Ventures of this order can be initiated, but they take a somewhat different form. A second type is the new product introduced to a familiar market in which present organizations operate. Using existing market organizations to supplement a new venture is an excellent approach, but should not be exploited until the venture enters the commercial development phase. New products that serve a market, either new to the company or utilizing its capabilities, represent a third type of product entry. Finally, a new product for the company as well as the market, for which no existing internal marketing apparatus is evident, becomes prime territory for New Venture Methodology.

Knowing the category of the venture product helps to define the extent and concentration of effort required. A product that is new to the company and the market relies on in-depth technical support. A product new to the company but not to the market should be, in part, innovative. Where the product is imitative, an imaginative approach must be relied upon. A product new to a familiar market has the best chance of success in the early stages. Avoidance of the overconfidence that comes with market familiarity should be paramount. Markets tend to be fickle and require continuous evaluation.

Preliminary Price Considerations

One of the other product—market relationships is the effect of pricing on sales. The theory of pricing covers many aspects of the analysis and should be considered during all phases of evaluation. Pricing as incorporated in the product discussion is somewhat less detailed than in the manufacturing and financial analyses. The price of the product must not exceed the price a customer will accept or can afford to pay for it. The latter is the ultimate value-in-use. The problem in this area is that the customer is often a heterogeneous group with a varying threshold described by a continuum line. Therefore one must select a price at a point or within a range on the line that achieves the desired level of sales. In Figure 38, stylized charts show the relationships of dollars in either income or profit as the price per unit of the venture product is increased. Total sales dollars will decrease as the price is increased, despite the greater income from each item (Graph A). Fewer items are sold at the higher prices, and this is generally not offset by the higher unit cost. At some very low price, the entire potential market should be captured. This, too, is theoretical. Some portion, due to alliances, allegiances, prejudices, or ignorance, will never be won over by the low price. Pragmatically, everyone assumes that when the low price is achieved something suffers, generally product quality. This results in a diminution of sales as described by the dotted line (Graph A). Sales in and of themselves are not the goal of business. It is profit from those sales to which our attention is given.

A curve describing the effect of price per unit on profits is shown in Graph B. At low unit pricing, no profit is achieved. But at some significant and definable point, profit is realized. Realistically, a loss

Figure 38. Pricing charts.

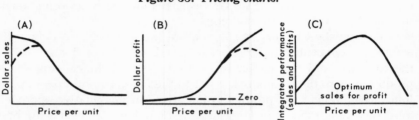

is incurred at the low prices, but since we are measuring profits, no negative values are shown. As price-per-unit increases, the potential profit increases to an optimum level. Theory says it goes on indefinitely, but ultimately, at some price, none of the product will be sold. The overall effect is the gradual loss of profits shown by the dotted line. Therefore, price must be considered seriously in the evaluation of the product. This doesn't mean that the optimum price will be charged, but that it should be defined. Pricing may be used to slow down early sales when there is limited production, and lowered to stimulate sales when capacity is available.

If one were to integrate the sales and profits curves at a specific time in the life cycle of the product, an optimum is seen (Graph C). Optimum price level is the one at which the best profitability occurs. The difficulty is that this approach deals with absolute profits. If percentage profits are desired, a higher price-per-unit would be selected to yield this. Sometimes it is desirable to reach a limited sales volume to effect other cost savings. As in any simple description, assumptions are made (for instance, that expenses are constant) that appear to be unrealistic. Later discussion on pricing considers these assumptions and influencing factors. It does not necessarily define an optimum price during the analysis of the venture product. Sophisticated pricing tools are used later in the delineation of the business strategy.

Product Specifications

The product specification document has been described as the single most important aspect of the product analysis and survey. The term has been an all-encompassing one, covering everything from the physical description of the product to intracompany contacts. On the other hand, a highly limiting definition can suffice where the additional data are collected using other analytical tools. The form then might be a technical data sheet or a modification for internal use. Within New Venture Methodology, the risk of duplication or overlap is minimized through the unidirectional and multidisciplinary approach of the single analyst or the small cadre of the initial team. In any case, it is better to have complete data with a degree of duplication than overlook a critical aspect in the product specification. It is also nothing more than a bookkeeping task to incorporate previously or concurrently developed data into the formal specification document. This is not duplication of effort but only duplication of recording. For these reasons, the product specification requirements outlined in this section have some redundancy and can be modified so that this is taken into account in actual practice.

A typical recommended product specification is shown in Figure 39. The format is general in nature and should always contain sufficient information with the appropriate amount of detail to serve as a giude for decision making and as an inclusion in the proposal for appropriating funds for venture development and commercialization. It is better to have a comprehensive document that can be used for various products and product types and for the stages of development than to design individualized forms for each product. The entries listed in Figure 39 start with a statement of the venture objective. This is put in the product specification to assure that there is immediate corroboration of the product's applicability to the objective of the venture. Although it may not be a requirement integral to the specification format, stating the objective does show the continuity from the recognition of the opportunity to its physical implementation.

The items that come next are informative for identifying the time of preparation, the individual preparing it, the project name if one is used, and the actual products that are being considered. The reason for listing the products is that there may be a product line involved that covers some allied but not necessarily similar items. The use of the product specification for more than one product in a product line is questionable. It is recommended that products be combined only when they have minimal or marginal differences. These similarities might come in the form of variations in size, color, style, or adornment. When the application is changed causing a change in the product description, even when the alteration is of a minor nature, a separate specification sheet is used. The problem encountered in combining several products in a single form is the need within several categories for special explanations to differentiate which entry goes with which product. Clarity and communication are required, which demands usage of many forms when several products are envisioned. With this as an accepted procedure, the successive data would then correspond to a single product. Obviously this simplifies the listing of physical characteristics.

While universality in format is preached, the entries remain specific for the individual product. There would be no need, for example, to cover the elastic properties of a material designed for a use in which absence or presence of such properties is totally inapplicable or of minute concern. Most characteristics will be defined in the product description covering technical and engineering properties. The features added in the physical-characteristics paragraph might be those subjective items that are important to visual evaluation or market acceptance but that are not related to some specific standards

Figure 39. Product specification.

Objective _____

Date _____

Project/analyst _____

Product (s) _____

Physical characteristics _____

_____

End uses, applications _____

_____

	Volume				
Pricing					
Sales, unit volume					

Competition

Products	Company	Price

Existing capabilities _____

_____

Design criteria _____

_____

Special considerations _____

_____

or test. It is critical to exclude items of peripheral importance. By definition, peripheral factors do not lend themselves to effectuating the decision or proposal. They are only interesting tidbits that are easily disregarded.

The end-use or applications entry can be a summation and condensation of the applications analysis. The additional input that might arise at this stage within the product specification could cover competing, supplemental, compatible, or coordinated internal products; internal options; type and attitude of the primary and ultimate consumer as well as changes in them. Verbalization should be concise and specific on the items related to product use, and should be subdivided into the projected applications areas. This can make a rather long list, and for this reason the best estimate of market size should be incorporated into the thinking. The result is a listing according to the magnitude of the market. The next two items are directly related to the application and, of course, to each other.

In product specification it is imperative that responsible estimates be used to describe pricing, volume, and sales in agreement with the ranges presented during the analysis steps. As part of a summation document, these items will have greater effect than they do in the detailed and extensive working documents. The theory of pricing and its relationship with the many planning and study stages culminate in the choice of some specific unit price figures for optimization of the venture. The anticipated sales, obviously an estimate that corresponds to time and new information, will be an updated inclusion. This is not a sales forecast, but it should be coordinated with the market projections with a comment as to when this level of sales is anticipated. The volume entry refers to the quantities required for volume prices.

Competition becomes a factor in the product judgment, and generally has implications of a high order of concern to management. A manager's primary interest in decision making is to know the competitive products, companies, and pricing policies in the market. Where none exist, it should be so stated. Potential competition or companies with latent capabilities would not be considered in the product specification. A footnote describing the patent situation of the parent company or of competition is a necessary addendum. Any proprietary or basic position disclosure would be reserved for documents used in planning and analysis. Existing capabilities of the company could be used to describe a proprietary position if a case could be made that they do truly represent an exceptionally outstanding or undeniably unique situation. Otherwise the existing capabilities should be viewed as physical, well-defined entities that are neither arbitrary nor controversial. They represent what can be done with current facilities, manpower, and organization.

Design criteria and special requirements comprise a miscellaneous entry that includes specific items that will be of significance to the product and its relation to the market. Especially noteworthy here are the need for changes in consumer practices and the need to educate customers and persuade them to make the change. Design criteria might also relate to tasks in support of sales that are derived from requests from customers for special items. The special-requirements section defines anticipated, unusual requests in terms of technical, manufacturing, or marketing factors. This should be confined to well-understood factors drawn from a multiplicity of sources during analysis. The important objective is balance, and the product specification should contain appropriate data in order to avoid either total rejection of the product or its being considered absolutely indispensable.

Product Testing

A short commentary on product testing is required to distinguish it from pretesting. The important difference is the direction of each type and the stage at which it is aimed. Product testing is carried out during research and development, often on a limited scale and frequently using methods scientifically designed to compare properties or gain precision. These tests eventually must be related to actual in-use performance. Accelerated testing would be another means of obtaining data that could be interpreted in terms of product life. Therefore, product testing occurs at an early stage of venture recognition, continuing to support the technical and engineering analyses. It is directed toward the product description and, perhaps, toward the accompanying data sheets or distributional literature required by the customer.

Product Pretesting

Pretesting differs from product testing in regard to the type of evaluation and the information sought. Pretesting is concerned with more practical properties. It exposes the product to pragmatic situations, or at least to conditions as close to the realistic end use as can be developed. Pretesting is usually carried out internally in one of three ways: (1) by using company facilities, (2) by using corporate employees, or (3) by artificially simulating conditions of actual use.

Using company facilities has several advantages and disadvantages. The advantages include a degree of security, better control, more flexibility, quicker response, and increased use of trained observers. On the debit side, there are problems of interdivisional communications, interference with ongoing business, early exposure to all levels of personnel, and a lack of proper priority. Using company personnel for testing presents some potential legal difficulties relating to responsibilities and damages. It also presupposes an amount of secrecy and a posture of objectivity. These qualities cannot be taken for granted in corporate employees. Also, the employees may not be representative of the actual users, and may hold some bias that skews the results. The final method for internal pretesting is to organize a test that imitates the user function, perhaps on a smaller scale. The obvious problems include the built-in bias, a chance of improper orientation, and an idealized, too-well-controlled attitude. Under some situations, internal pretesting of a product can be so totally endemic that it becomes invalid. The best approach for venturing is to do a small amount of this prior to external pretesting.

The key decision is the choice of external group for this type of evaluation. Judgments are usually more realistic, less likely to be specious, and, when a need exists, evaluators can be highly cooperative, interested, and contributory. Of course, one is displaying to those selected users a new product before moving into the market. Security may or may not be jeopardized. The venturer will also have to live with his shortcomings and reveal them to a potential customer. Therefore, the choice of external pretesting sites, organizations, and people is critical, as is an understanding but not apologetic pretester. There are five categories to consider: (1) existing customers, (2) established customers, (3) potential customers, (4) recoverable customers, and (5) intransigent users.

Existing and established customers. Existing customers include any companies, organizations, or individuals with whom the parent company does business—new and old, good and bad, large and small, interested and uninterested. Perhaps some will be potential customers if the venture development is successful. Established customers could be very friendly, long-term users of other corporate products, or those presently using a similar material or product that you seek to supplant. These people would probably be the easiest to work with, but as the only pretesters, since they may be too kind.

Potential customers. Potential customers are undoubtedly the best to work with in most cases. Their interest is high, their need should be definable and real, and the rewards to them are easily recognizable. The additional benefit that accrues is that sales can quickly blossom upon successful demonstration of the product. As a caution, supply of the successful new product must be planned in order not to deny, delay, or frustrate these customers.

Recoverable customers. Recoverable customers are those who have dealt with some part of the company at some time in the past and have elected to purchase elsewhere. The venture that uses this kind of organization to work with the new product generally has ulterior motives tied to sales. Sparing use of these operations is recommended, in that a spectrum of different contributors can be helpful provided that only a nominal effort is expended on such potential customers.

Intransigent users. This is perhaps a strong term. It could include present or potential users of products similar to the new product in question. Basically they no doubt will have some reason for rejecting dealings with the parent company because of obligations such as to their own internal source of a competitive product, or a commitment to equipment not suitable for modification. Although it might be helpful to develop some rapport and sales insight might be gained, this is not the best climate or the optimum candidate for pretesting. It is better to choose sites and people that will provide a good sampling, where need motivates, where feedback of information is maximized and reliability is excellent. These data will be the foundation upon which successive field testing will be based.

Field Testing

The first active step that highlights and magnifies the performance and acceptance of the product is the field test. This might be the prelude to market testing, or it can be concurrent with it since it serves both purposes. Field testing should not be relegated to a position as a casual or routine procedure to satisfy some managerial whim. It is an information-gathering process, and is part of the venture cycle which, in its orientation to the venture product, does not neglect the peripheral benefits. To gain maximum benefit, certain points should be given attention. The first is the task of recording, or reducing results and ancillary information to writing for immediate and future reference and arranging them into disciplinary groupings. Evaluation that determines the pertinence, reliability, and accuracy of the data follows. Interpretation, which judges their significance in relation to other, previously derived information, enables conclusions to be drawn in various areas of interest to the venture.

In evaluating the results of field testing, one should give pertinence of product performance data first-order consideration. The immediacy of the need for data, the information required for future decision making, and the manpower needs for testing are elements that affect the degree of relevance. Reliability is a sensitive area, and it must be rated on the basis of actual experience and personal judgment. Knowledge of how sophisticated the trial operation or user is, of the people's training and attitudes, of their management's degree of commitment, and of the criteria of the testers' capabilities will all be factored into the reliability evaluation. A rating chart could be applied to specific data or the individual user in the field test. A table for labeling each of these can be drawn up to insure consistency among the analysts in the field.

RATING	MEANING
I	Completely reliable data
II	Usually reliable data
III	Fairly reliable data
IV	Partially reliable data
V	Reliability not judged

This is not a progressive scale, and the use of verbal descriptions is stressed, the numbers being used only for reference. Where control, confidence, experience, and knowledge are optimized, a rating of I is possible. Lesser ratings would be applied for reasons noted by the analyst. Unreliable data should not be considered and needs no rating symbol.

Accuracy is a probability function evaluated on the basis of internal consistency of reporting, precision of observation, agreement among observers, and talents of the testers. A table to rate accuracy can also be used by the risk group evaluators.

RATING	DEFINITION
A	95–100% ; reproducibly demonstrated
B	85–95% ; highly probable, demonstrated
C	75–85% ; probable, inferred
D	50–75% ; possible, assumed
E	Accuracy not judged

An A rating indicates a high degree of accuracy judged on the basis of a use situation that was reproducibly demonstrated, properly recorded, observed, and confirmed. For a B accuracy rating a single demonstration might suffice to reach this conclusion. This does not necessarily mean merely a single trial but, where multiple properties are being evaluated, some properties may not be analyzed as thoroughly or repetitively as others. At times, use of a new product might be demonstrated with certain factors inferred from the general success. Here a C rating might be assigned. Some doubt falls on the value of tests or the accuracy of trials in which a D rating is given. The fewer assumptions made, the lower is the ultimate risk for venture success. In some cases no judgment of data accuracy is made, and data the nature of which is undefined should be used for confirmatory purposes only.

Finally, field-testing data must be sifted and sorted to isolate the key points. Emphasis is placed on the critical data elements as they relate to analyses previously prepared. The total effort is then integrated to give a logical picture of the capability and functionality of the product in the field. More than one conclusion might be possible, which should have a negative influence on the validity of the product's readiness for the market. The final deductions are formulated on the basis of the collected and recorded data verifying the existence of a viable business opportunity.

Other Product Tests

Several other means of testing the viability or friability of the venture product assist in reaching the proper business decision about it. Three examples are consumer panels, trade shows, and exposure through announcements, advertisements, releases, and new-product bulletins. Consumer panels are generally applicable for products used in the form in which they will be sold. They are useful for products aimed at a nonspecific market with a size of reasonable magnitude. Panel tests tend to deal directly with the marketability and the in-use functionality of the product. The statistical aspects are important. The type of panel chosen, the proper sampling, the number of panels, the questions asked, the use of comparatives, and the imposed economic limits of the venture-testing budget play a role in the contribution of the panels. Caution should be exercised because it is too easy to influence results by inappropriate choices among these factors. The talents to carry out these tests may not be available within the risk group, and therefore professional assistance should be seriously considered. This type of testing is complex, and while many consumer-oriented businesses have become extremely proficient in the use of panels, they can be misleading in amateurs' hands.

Trade shows can be used to take the pulse of specific industrial acceptance. Some limitations to this technique detract from the good features, which include external information, names of people interested in your product, comments from knowledgeable sources, and general marketing and merchandising input. Once a product is displayed, it is necessary to be able to send samples or deliver orders promptly thereafter. Delays or inability to supply in short order can be discouraging if not disastrous. While exposure is helpful in generating early sales, it also reveals one's intentions openly and early enough to become vulnerable to competitors. The showing is for market-testing purposes. Competitors are alert to new developments and, of course, they will have become quite aware of a new operational direction. In addition to those people interested in gaining intelligence and filling their needs, a large number of extraneous and superfluous questions, comments, requests, and opinions will accrue. This adds to the time-consuming nature of participating in trade shows, since proper attention must be given to all inquiries during and after the show.

The effort to review, sort, select, and weigh becomes greater when considerable academic curiosity is added to the truly interested requests. Of course, the quantity of those truly interested is highly pertinent information but a large degree of casual interest can result in dichotomy. Another consideration in using trade shows is the expense. Not that it is any more expensive than other methods for information gathering, but the cost is easily underestimated. Hidden costs are often extensive and exceed the obvious expenditures. Superficial cost estimates for trade shows should be viewed suspiciously. Finally, the specificity of the group at any one show often requires venture participation in several shows. While overlap can occur, industry appeal and geographic boundaries must be considered to insure proper sampling.

Products or services are the focal point in the business opportunity. Analyses revolve around the product as it is related to the technical, manufacturing, marketing, and financial disciplines. The proposal, the organization, the investment, the commercialization all find their basis in the character and ultimate utilization of the product. Because the product is the central factor, the time and effort expended on all the considerations outlined here, and on those that might be added in light of the specific product and situation, are not only pertinent but necessary.

7

The Proposal

In New Venture Methodology, the preparatory efforts culminate in venture development. In order to move into this phase, many requirements must be completed. Among these are extensive planning, search and selection, and various analyses. Each has been discussed in detail as guides to most effectively selecting the lowest-risk and highest-reward venture. The organization plays a role in this selection, and of course its recognition of the product introduced by the venture is necessary. All these details, documentation, and study must be brought to the attention of corporate management since it makes the final decision and will supply the venture capital.

It is an oversimplification to assume that such an intensified effort of data gathering and evaluation could proceed without gradual involvement of management at increasingly higher levels. The key decision makers will be kept informed at least in part by the informal organization as well as through their required participation during certain phases of the venture study. They will not, however, have been exposed to the formal documents, which means they will be less than fully informed on the integrated components of the opportunity study. The matter addressed in this chapter is the recommended mechanism for accomplishing the task of informing management and requesting action and support to move into the market.

It helps in the preparation and the review if a fixed and accepted format is used, for in every case, extenuating circumstances arise and the format is altered to fit the individual venture proposition. This only helps to support the desire for a stable base of departure. The

131

format used is not simply an appropriation requisition form, but a more complete document that supports the request for funds. A formal appropriation form has an important function and is required by many organizations in order to simplify and clarify decision making. It is often highly financial in nature, and distills those features that a particular executive committee feels are needed to reach the proper decision. Such a form, or a short, formal request, does not, however, represent a thorough enough proposal when a new business venture of any consequence is being considered. Most appropriation forms do satisfy the needs of the decision makers when buildings, equipment, or some other capital expenditure is involved for a specified objective.

In a venture, the questions are broader and more extensive and require detailed information to satisfy management because more major dollar outlays are to be made. An oral proposal accompanying the appropriation request form may suffice, but the written document serves to allow preview and study and provides a historical record. It is the charter for the new business, and collects in one entity the efforts, data, assumptions, and conclusions accumulated up to this critical decision point, prior to venture development. It should be recalled that a major commitment of funds is not required until the venture reaches the commercialization stage. When discussing the stages of a venture, it is recommended that funds for venture development be requested as a formality, and they should be readily allotted barring any major deficiencies. If the venture is small relative to the corporation's size, the proposal is really for information only, since it is understood that the venture will proceed at the judgment of the risk group manager. The proposal, therefore, is the key document. The request for additional funds, if it is required at this point in lieu of directing budgeted funds into venture development, is a secondary consideration. The proposal is the report to management and supplies general internal intelligence across various line responsibilities.

The form we propose here may seem excessively long and may contain some relatively noncritical categories. It is admittedly a thorough and somewhat arbitrary selection of categories. There is some apparent duplication, and it includes items not previously described in the paragraphs covering planning and analysis. Certain items and categories are perhaps more applicable to a given organization than others and should be chosen according to the judgment of the venture leader preparing the integrated proposal. An outline, shown at the end of the chapter, covers the elements of the proposal. The next section discusses the details.

Organizing the Document

The Executive Summary

This is probably the most important and specifically directed portion of the proposal. It is written for general management only. This management may be an executive committee, the president, the chief operating officer, or whoever the ultimate decision maker or makers are in the company. It is not for peripheral and line managers or staff vice-presidents. It should not be written for the administrative chain in which the venture operation is housed. The most common error is to write and rewrite it in response to remarks from each level of reviewing management.

Although it was recommended that the venture group report to the highest possible managerial level, in practice it does not always work out this way. If it is necessary to violate this tenet, the single most devastating violation would be to allow anyone other than the venture leader to prepare the proposal. He is the incipient entrepreneur who has the total picture in complete focus. If he doesn't, perhaps the wrong man was chosen. For intermediary administrators to attempt to influence the content of the document by other than passive advice can cause two future problems. First, statements might be imposed upon the entrepreneur for which he may have no enthusiasm or in fact with which he may disagree. The second complication is the increased chance for misunderstanding at a later date, when the reporting chain has changed and the venture leader has direct contact with the evaluators and decision makers. Consistency and compatibility between this proposal and the future request for appropriations to go commercial must be maintained to insure the support of management. The proposal is also instructive and constructive for the venture leader in his continual planning and in monitoring the progress of the venture.

The summary should contain several segments to give, in staccato fashion, the key factors of the venture plan. The opportunity should be described verbally, including numbers on total market, potential and percentage of penetration. The product of the business contemplated has to be discussed in terms of type, number, volume, and mix. Constructs of the market and the time required to reach portions of it, the influence of competition, and general product status should be concisely stated. The question as to why the company should be in the business concerned requires an answer. By putting the answer in the executive summary, one avoids the obvious questions and eliminates possible areas of objection. An appropriation of funds is required when the decision to proceed is accepted. Therefore it is encumbent on the venturer to state what monies are to be spent. This explicit request for dollars can then be followed by a general statement as to what the funds will buy in tangible and intangible items. With these data, a reasonable abstract of the business is in the hands of the corporate hierarchy.

The Introduction

This is the most flexible section of the proposal. It can contain such background material as the historical development, the tasks completed, the techniques used, and the important content references. The introduction can express some of the opinions or intuitive comments by reviewing administrative management. It should also be kept short; a moderate-sized paragraph should be adequate. The venture leader must retain responsibility for this section, but he should allow input from other major sources to broaden the business concept, give depth to the subject, imply flexibility of approach, and present decision-making points. This should not be viewed as an allowable intrusion by intermediate management to influence the content of the introduction. It should reflect only their support.

Corporate Objectives

As is the case for both the summary and the introduction, the objectives should be stated on a separate page. This serves to remind general management of the corporate objectives as they apply to this situation, and shows how the venture leader interprets them. It presents the specific aspects of these objectives in the long and short range and states how this venture will accomplish them. It is expeditious at this juncture to restate and reinforce the general management commitment by quoting its directives and attitudes toward new-business development, toward this area of interest, and toward this venture.

Market Research

This is not to be a reiteration of the available or in-progress market research data. The point to be made here is that the decision makers want to know that the market has been studied and understood. To them, knowing that a survey was run internally, that outside sources corroborate the results, that a staff organization is participating, and that consultants or independent organizations have advised positively, are more important than the actual results. If conclusions can be stated numerically and concisely, they can be of additional value. There is no need to make market research conclusions the key feature of the paragraph. The importance of building confidence in conclusions throughout the proposal is critical, and the reliability and credibility of the sources are more important than the actual detailed data. This proposal is a management document, and the data that support it can be made readily available or supplied as addenda if necessary.

Economic Studies

The least readable but most understandable aspects of new-business development are the economic implications. Few comments will be needed here except where assumptions not normally anticipated are made or where they are specific for the proposed venture. The important documents come from the financial analysis, and would describe the revenues from various income sources, the projected total invoiced sales during the stated time period, the costs of manufacture and other expenses, the investment requirements initially and projected for the successful venture, and the ROI yardstick or whichever measure might be most applicable to the individual company. It would be best to develop some short form for the financial analysis charts, rather than use them in full for this initial proposal. As experience allows, the financial portion will be updated by the risk group. Precise and accurate financial information, including longer-term projections, is eventually required prior to venture commercialization. At that point a plan and request for commercialization will be prepared and presented. The detailed financial data, against which operational performance will be measured, would be made available as a requisite part of the plan hopefully compatible with the data presented in the proposal.

Budget

While the paragraph on economic studies was described as a preliminary summary for the purposes of this proposal, the budget assumes different proportions. There is need for the budget to be carefully adhered to during the life of the venture development. It should be detailed in dollar expenditures, items, and timing. A month-by-month chart for the one- to two-year period of venture development as described in the financial analysis is a minimum requirement. The categories should include all contingencies and should realistically show allotted funds. Conservative estimates of expenses can lead to overoptimistic and nonachievable levels of performance, whereas overestimation of expenses may result in overspending, a false sense of security, or incorrect impressions of the real needs.

Organization

Remarks on organization should be concise and specific. Although a stylized chart is helpful, it should be added only for impact. To the reader, the more critical concerns are how many people will be needed, what type of jobs will be executed, where the people will come from, and how they will be administered. The growth in organization and near-term modifications or reorientations in personnel can be described. Organizational structure in disciplines substantially different from those normally anticipated by the reviewing management can be either graphically or verbally described.

Facilities

Tangible items often gain the most attention and are the easiest to discuss at length and in depth. This should be avoided, since the object of the proposal is to familiarize general management with the facts, not bore them with elaborate descriptive prose. While Figure 39 shows a long list of items, these are readily combined in a few short sentences. Cost, type, space, and location are clear cut. The time of occupancy of a facility coincides with the plans for the overall venture development. The decision to rent or purchase should be stated with a justification in mind. The proposal should indicate how the facilities and the production capacity, which may change with time, can be utilized. Although showing a blueprint or picture of a new facility in an oral presentation is valuable to demonstrate the extent of the thinking and planning done on this subject, it should not be a part of the proposal. In no case does the proposal serve in lieu of the actual detailed planning and action documents, nor should it include them.

Product

The executive summary has laid the groundwork in its superficial description of the product, its mix, and the market served. The best way to describe the product clearly is to display a prototype or a manufactured, finished item. This cannot be put into the proposal. Neither are the complete written specifications and technical, manufacturing, and engineering details a necessary part of the proposal. However, there may be some need for a better description of the product than the one the executive summary affords. One brief paragraph can expand and clarify the product concept. Because the product is the central feature of the business, it gains much attention and interest. Where further data are deemed important and should be included, an annex of data sheets might be a separate enclosure. A statement in the proposal that these have been prepared on the basis of specific testing or evaluations is really all that is required. A discussion of raw materials may or may not be included, depending upon its potential impact on the corporation or the project. Corporate management is often intrigued by the forward integration of existing products, which should be considered important enough to include in this section. Don't, however, present it out of proportion to its actual contribution to the venture or the company. Of course, when forward integration is active, with a synergistic effect valuable to the corporation, it should be presented.

One might also include comments on market needs in relation to proprietary or patented practices and concepts. Although all these points may be pertinent, their relative importance should be weighed and reflected in the extent of coverage given them.

Pricing

A price sheet is probably the best way to disclose prices in the proposal, but it is not easily read nor does it highlight the key factors. Comments on price range, the effect of size or volume, and the influence of sales strategies should therefore be included in the discussion. Competition practices or industry standards can also be included for comparative evaluation. Value added, the margin above manufacturing cost and/or value-in-use, contributes to the overall picture.

The critical point again is to indicate clearly that accurate, detailed work has gone into this activity. Background details can then be made available upon request or discussed orally when some specific, crucial point is brought to light. Persuasive discussion to avoid management interdiction should not be needed at this initial proposal stage. Confidence in the venture leader should be high enough that management accepts justification without requiring detailed disclosure.

Strategy

Sales strategy is a complex undertaking. The basis for such strategy must be developed in the field under actual selling conditions. The market analysis has revealed the fundamental points and given direction to the venture. This is a good place to propose a projected sales volume, the need for training sales personnel in the new field of endeavor, the geographic plan for distributing the number of salesmen, and the identification of customers. The detail must await further field experience.

The object in going through a venture development phase is to induce coordination among various functions and to define the proper route to the marketplace. A sales strategy that comes from actual field contacts will grow and mature as the business climate and customer attitudes are fed into the system from the line personnel. While sales strategy is formative at this stage, it is imperative that it become a structured plan prior to venture commercialization.

Alternatives

Presenting rejected alternatives to the chosen venture in a proposal is at best controversial. Management will assume that various courses have been developed and the most appropriate one chosen. Once the decision is made, the venture leader has committed himself and the risk group to the selection upon which the proposal is based. It may assist corporate management to be made aware of the decision-making process that evaluated several possible courses of action. While alternatives may exist, they are only academically interesting. Pragmatically, they are eliminated by the proposal for one best approach, and their inclusion tends to dilute the force of the proposal. To mention that alternatives were viewed and the best one was chosen can allay fears that other avenues might have been overlooked. To be specific is detrimental, since it is impossible to catalog all alternatives, let alone explain and reject them. Someone can always find a unique alternative that was not listed in the proposal. For these reasons, alternatives should be discussed only when exigencies are anticipated. If venture development is undertaken on the basis of self-imposed limitations for convenience during the trial-and-learning phase, future alternatives can be stated. Alternatives in the initial proposal phase are of the "what if" variety, chosen on the basis of various degrees of success of a product or several forms of it from which a selection is planned. Refer to alternative venture choices with discretion, since it can complicate more than clarify when the venture development has a single best path to follow.

Special Considerations

To attempt discussion of various items that may be relegated to a paragraph on special considerations would be folly. Specific requirements, or lack of them, for each venture will be obvious to the venture leader. While patents of competitors or legal matters might be special considerations, the fact that they are special means that they will be dealt with in appropriate sections in the proposal.

References and Bibliography

This section is reserved for the answers to all those anticipated and detail-seeking questions. It would be inappropriate to attach a volume of documents and worksheets, reports and articles, patents and data sheets. This can be avoided by preparing a list of those supporting documents that contributed to the development of the proposal. The actual documents can become part of a file copy or placed in a central working file that becomes the authoritative reference for the venture and its personnel. The importance of this section is to call attention to the in-depth effort expended. It should not be padded, or contain extraneous references that misdirect, dilute, or complicate the intent of the proposal since they would remain part of it.

Presentation, Distribution, and Approval

A few matters that are not necessarily inherent parts of the proposal deal with convenience, coverage, distribution, and approvals or authentications. One minor point that adds to the general professional manner of presentation is the cover. A formal cover designed specifically for venture proposals is advisable. Where several proposals are continually in process, the cost of special covers is easily justified. When the proposal is a one-time item, as may be the case for a small company or an individual entrepreneur, a first-class, decorative cover gives the impression of an effort made with a mature, professional approach and attention to detail. The same is true of any attached figures. The few hours of effort or the few dollars expended are easily worth the impression made by the visual quality of the proposal.

Obviously, a proposal is written for a body of people who will receive individual copies. However, others may need to see the proposal and can contribute as a result of being informed. They should be included in a later distribution, after management's acceptance of the proposal. A record should be kept of those receiving a copy. Both venture team members and assisting staff should also preview the proposal if possible, especially within their areas of expertise and contribution. They may receive copies whether the proposal is approved or not. In all cases, the copies should be dated and authenticated by the author so no mistakes about improper or preliminary copies will be revealed at a later date.

The final stage is the approval. Frequently, members of the approving committee do not affix their signatures but use some other mechanism to show their approval. A paragraph should then be written by the proposal's author describing who, when, where, and under what circumstances the approval was given. This is added to each transmitted copy so that everyone is aware of the corporate commitment.

The proposal is an important document as a point of decision. Earlier decisions to proceed with investigating the opportunity have been made at the initial screening, during comparative selection, and within several separate analyses. All of these lead to the decision to initiate venture development. The proposal enables the venture leader to inform and request, permits management to be informed, to authorize, and to commit, and is the means by which the risk group is guided and can act. Implementation of the venture plan, summarized in part by the proposal, is the important task; the proposal is the beginning, not the finale, of the venture action.

Proposal Outline

   I. Executive summary
     A. Opportunity
     B. Product
     C. Market, timing
     D. Corporate role
     E. Appropriation required
     F. What the appropriation will buy

  II. Introduction

 III. Corporate Objectives (specific)
     A. Short term
     B. Long term
     C. Mission of this venture group
     D. Management's directives
     E. Management's attitudes

 IV. Market research
     A. Source, reliability
     B. Time, depth
     C. Key features
     D. Corporate fit

V. Economic studies
   A. Consolidated income
   B. Sales projection
   C. Expenses
   D. Investment
   E. ROI yardstick

VI. Budget
   A. Timing
   B. Detail

VII. Organization
   A. Number of people
   B. Growth
   C. Type of structure
   D. Source of people
   E. Administration
   F. Job descriptions

VIII. Facilities
   A. Cost
   B. Type
   C. Space
   D. Utilization
   E. Location
   F. Growth
   G. Rent/purchase
   H. Timing
   I. Volume of production

IX. Product
   A. Description
   B. Source of raw materials
   C. Needs
   D. Data sheets
   E. Competition
   F. Patents or proprietary position

X. Pricing
   A. Distribution
   B. Volume
   C. Value-in-use

XI. Strategy
   A. Sales
   B. Training
   C. Geographics
   D. Timing

8

The Business Strategy

WITHIN New Venture Methodology the venture development phase has manifold objectives. Whereas the inception phase encompassed the search, screening, and selection, and the analysis phase culminated in a product and a proposal, venture development is the first stage of action. Implementation of the plans, initiation of marketing, verification of the opportunity, and setting up the business strategy according to which the commercial stage is entered are not only anticipated consequences but specific goals. The purpose of venture development is to set the stage for commercialization and to supply those needs for making the right decisions.

Venture Development

Plans are prepared for small-lots manufacturing, for field testing and initial sales encounters, and for examination of the details of the venture proposal. The learning process will precede decision making, and some limits must be placed on the venture development time. It is advisable to be reasonable about the time taken during the proposal preparation. A good length of time to allow for investigating a venture project prior to commercialization is a maximum of one year. The suggested technique, however, is to set up decision points at particular segments of the development of the opportunity. These can then be periodically summarized, perhaps on a quarterly basis, to describe the status of the business development.

At six-month intervals, key points should be reached that present a choice of three alternatives. Alternative 1 would be a decision to obtain data and experience, following the initial plan on schedule. This implies continued venture development with a proposal to commercialize at the second six-month increment. Alternative 2 would be to suggest to management a modified approach on the basis of practical experience. When the change does not dramatically affect the timetable and it appears that commercialization will proceed on schedule or close to it, no real problems should occur. The acceptance of the altered direction is routine, and the reporting function has been fulfilled.

Alternative 3 is dual in nature. If the response in the marketplace is better than anticipated, a modified plan might be required. Understandably, it is preferable when customers place orders for the product or sign contracts for the service offered. But customer reaction that is merely positive, pleasant, or encouraging would not constitute a reponse of sufficient magnitude to justify varying plans. These changes usually result in increased expenditures, higher capital outlay sooner than originally designated, and, in fact, earlier commercialization. Manufacturing would be rapidly expanded, which might be tedious or impossible. High-volume production from small lots or pilot-plant units is frequently uneconomical. Success is the goal, but even that can have negative ramifications. In any case, if a decision to capitalize on the early success is warranted, then it should be made. The six-month reporting period is designed to allow for this. Some ventures, by virtue of their simplicity or complexity, may not be assessed as one-year venture development potentials. They can have somewhat different time scales. It is not easy to envision a shorter development phase for a venture of any consequence. On the other hand, holding a venture in the evaluation and development phase too long is uneconomical and might be the consequence of overambition, poor planning, or a venture with a questionable chance for success.

The second option of alternative 3, if it is an option and not an obvious route, is to reassess the venture's possibility of success. All too often, a move is made prematurely to extend the time period. This should be avoided, except according to the second alternative. Once it is recognized that the additional time requested is beyond a moderate extension and that it may not result from a change in plans but from a failure to meet them, a clearer decision process can follow. With the data obtained, the various components of the original analysis should be reexamined. If remedial action is plausible, a situation recurs paralleling the second alternative described above. When no straightforward solution can be found, the venture must be recognized as a nonbusiness in its current form and must be rejected, no matter how difficult that is to do.

To maintain a high-risk, low-confidence venture is the antithesis of New Venture Methodology. It is not easy to terminate a venture or come out unscathed, but in a case like this it must be done. If it appears that success is still possible but requires more extensive examination and new input, whether technical, manufacturing, or marketing, another approach can be used. This also applies to ventures in which the rewards are potentially great and the concept has not suffered in the derogation of the initial goal. Here the venture can revert to a research or product-development stage to reorient the product or derive some new functional item to do the job. If this is not the problem, engineering research to decrease cost or redesign the product may be in order.

If there are no technical difficulties and it is not necessary to go back to the drawing board, the business can be retained as a possible venture. The analysis can be redone with new information and perhaps with a change in direction. This should not be done while venture development continues unabated. It may seem overly courageous or even foolhardy to shut off the venture with the hope of reinstituting it later. In many corporations, this is venture suicide. However, it is better than clinging to a loser that saps funds from better-priority risks or better ventures. If the new analysis leads to a new proposal, the start should be fresh and the direction clearly delineated from previous attempts. Retreaded ventures have sour tastes for management, entrepreneurs, and organization members, and an early rejection is a superior alternative to continual regurgitation

Preparing the Strategy

The business strategy is the groundwork for commercialization. It is developed during the venture development stage. It helps in making decisions since it is the basis for the allocation of funds. When venture commercialization is approved, the first major appropriations for both capital and working investments are committed. The components of the business strategy are isolated from previous considerations made on the basis of general information and compatibility with corporate goals, policies, procedures, and plans.

Marketing

The first and most important part of the data acquired through venture development activities is the marketing information. Sales strategy is not fixed prior to the venture proposal presentation; it is the first job undertaken during venture development. Forecasts for planning purposes will be set but they are not sacrosanct. The need to adjust them according to a new strategy is inherent in this mobile phase. Sales are critical and should be separated clearly from any testing or test marketing that does not represent a typical, standard, or expected consumer action. Sales should be forecast on a month-by-month basis during venture development. Projections for following years can be shown on a yearly basis, since monthly forecasts beyond one year are shaky approximations at best. When variations become major, perhaps a 25 percent deviation from that projected, explanation and justification are required. The customers stand within the context of sales projections. They might be different in kind or type than anticipated.

Customers may be located in different geographic areas. Their relative volumes of purchases could be different than those originally projected. When one is dealing with geographics, several approaches might be followed. Maintaining intensified coverage of a single market region might prove most satisfactory for the products involved. Alternately, a less saturating approach, still within the confines of a local geographic area, might be better. This is often required when the list is limited and customers are geographically scattered. In diverse market situations, other strategies may be more appropriate.

The method used to reach the market is worthy of attention. The sales organization can spiderweb out as sales areas are extended, expanding outward from a central point. This allows controlled growth with maximum administrative and supervisory efficiency. An alternate method might be to let the sales force leapfrog from one core area to another, each sustaining its own small web of activity. But this raises problems of diminished control, higher expenses, and greater strains on distributional facilities in cost and control. Yet it is preferable to the random demographic approach, which concerns the major population centers without giving proper attention to the value of such areas in sales per expense dollar. This method may be used if national exposure is desired, or for nationally known and distributed consumer products that adhere to demographic use patterns.

This raises the matter of regional versus national marketing. For ventures that must start national in scope, risk and costs are disproportionately magnified. This does not eliminate them as good business opportunities, but it does require a more experienced sales force and management. It also means early sophistication in pricing, although an opportunity to acquire it may not be readily available. Small misestimations can be costly in underprice dollar losses or overprice sales misses. When pricing is understood on a local basis and a regional approach selected, customers must be clearly identified and rated for priority attention.

The problem of big customers versus small ones in usage and sales dollars is not resolved simply. Although dealing with larger customers gives rapid, single-contact sales, there are disadvantages. Often more calls are needed. A greater degree of technical backup is required. Decision time is not always as rapid as that of the smaller consumer. Price breaks or discounts for volume are expected. Large orders might strain the manufacturing facilities before they are in operation or up to a reasonable production capacity. There is also less margin for error. One error has enormous consequences and could result in total rejection by an entire industry. It works to the seller's advantage to deal with smaller customers, making it easier to respond to their needs and correct errors. And the risk is spread over several potential users. If the economics of doing business with the large customer are overwhelming, taking small steps with them is recommended. They in turn may enforce such action, resulting in a commitment and time to react to it that are dual protections against overexposure.

The advice is to choose the minimum-risk situation to conserve capital. Hence, where possible, venture development should operate from a regional sales base, expanding in a spiderweb pattern, dealing with smaller customers of the minimum size necessary to achieve meaningful results.

Product Strategy

All aspects of marketing will, of course, affect the business strategy, and some would contend that all parts of a business influence marketing. However, the product has been handled separately in this book to more clearly delineate its effect upon the opportunity. The field, where the product is in the hands of the customer, is the ultimate proving ground for a product's performance. All the in-house tests and preliminary definitions must stand the test of the user, since he makes the buying decision. Venture development hinges on the critical pin of performance. It is not always a singular feature or a predictable property that controls the result. For this reason, among others, extreme care and specific attention must be given to in-use results. Reorders are usually good indicators, but nothing replaces detective work at all levels to ferret out any shortcomings. Products that may develop long-term problems are most difficult to judge if the venture adheres to a one-year development program.

Equally important to the product's performance is its presentation. Public relations releases can have a positive effect on sales calls and, hopefully, on sales. Releases must be accurate and descriptive. The choice of publications to be sent the release is important. False leads waste time and money. Also, a technical product in a lay journal may so miss the desired customer that the effort is wasted. Publicity releases should be tied into advertising and directly related to sales goals. Using this technique merely to develop a scrapbook or satisfy someone's ego is not only haphazard but detrimental to serious venturing.

Advertising plays an important part in venture development. It requires cash outlays, and is controlled directly by the venture leader, who is responsible for expenditures. Funds are usually limited. The venture goals to be accomplished through advertising are either foggy or exceedingly narrow. It is used more for highlighting a local campaign or testing the impact of a type, style, or amount of advertising than to accomplish in-depth sales. The object of venture development is not to maximize sales but to optimize them, so limited, directed advertising is involved. Therefore, the public relations releases and advertising should be geared to those limited objectives set for near-term achievement.

Other important product tools include properly designed and available literature, impressive packaging, and a means of exposing the product to the purchaser and the ultimate customer. The latter refers to such events as trade shows, industry showings, and other similar public or private presentations. The use of literature as a sales tool is well known. How it is used in the business strategy may be somewhat unique to the venture product. It shows that in the venture development stage, the venture staff has studied the requirements for well-designed material. The costs of some pieces can be high and choices must be made concerning priority, applicability, and results. It is better to limit the number and produce a piece of high quality that supplies usable and pertinent information, even at the expense of descriptive sales verbiage. The basis for producing such literature is laid during the venture development phase.

Packaging is primarily a functional element, though under appropriate circumstances its impact on sales can be significant. No doubt packaging will be vulnerable to continuous change, but the concept and requirements for a given package will be developed prior to commercialization. From this, a strategy will be built to include all portions of the product presentation.

Trade shows help to expose the product to a broad range of people while still limiting and defining the audience. They can be quite helpful in the initial stages of venture development, but they are time consuming and expensive and should be undertaken only when specific objectives are sought and can be realized. One of the requirements is certainly a programmed approach. This is requisite not only during development, but after commercialization is entered. Because the preparation is extensive and the time required, in terms of personnel committed, is substantial, trade show and exhibits should not be treated lightly. By planning smaller and more localized ones, cost and exposure can be controlled, although this appears to be recessive. If coverage and exposure are desired, the best approach is to concentrate one's efforts on one or two important, well-attended conventions. At such times it is wise not to oversell the product, present unavailable items, or make commitments that should be reserved for sales calls. It is advisable to evaluate critically all results emanating from the exhibition. It is easy to become overambitious and superoptimistic in the climate of a trade-show booth. Used to learn as well as to sell, this approach has a place in the business strategy and can be viewed in its proper perspective.

The manufacturing operation is one that has caused many problems in new-product development for innumerable companies. No product is going to succeed in the marketplace if it cannot be reproducibly manufactured at quantities required by the market and within the predefined economic limits. In light of the aggressive financial and marketing approach of new ventures, to neglect this critical aspect can prove disastrous. Experience shows that this happens all too frequently, and lack of delivery or delivery of poor-quality material spells potential failure. The only way to avoid this is to be sure a workable process is in hand before venture development is initiated.

It is also incumbent upon the venture leader to coordinate commitments to sales, with production capability. Proving this capability in a small pilot operation reinforces the faith the venture people have in their process. The decision to make the product precursors such as raw materials or component parts or to purchase them can be made early, allowing time to reevaluate it as development proceeds. Wherever possible, purchasing components at the small-lots levels is preferable. But only through internal small-lots production can the elements of cost be critically examined. Product cost as a function of the sales projections, that is, the volume or scale of productivity, can be estimated with some degree of accuracy. As growth and expansion of the business moves smoothly, a continuous, uninterrupted supply of the product is required to support sales endeavors. Not only is manufacturing cost verified by continuous production, but the investment in equipment for commercialization will become apparent. The facilities and their location should be part of the business detail outlined in the strategy. These data are important and should be analyzed critically as sales patterns evolve.

Finally, quality control must receive proper attention. The risk in ignoring or subordinating quality control is too great, in the earlier stages, to accept. Two items that any venture should focus on in the manufacturing area are: (1) the production of quality items, reproducibly and in sufficient quantity to satisfy sales, and (2) the critical and realistic definition of production costs, present and projected.

Distribution is understood most readily when the actual movement of the product is involved. Shipping costs can be read from charts, but the many hidden aspects show up in practice. Crating or palletizing may be overlooked in original estimates. Disproportionate costs of small orders must be taken into account. Costs for labels, special services, and insurance are often underrated in general estimates. The market may warrant warehousing to achieve efficiencies in distribution. Space costs may be the smallest item when fees for paperwork, materials handling, sorting, or selecting are involved. If distribution centers are needed, the strategy must include money and plans for space, locations, personnel, and equipment to service a satellite operation or warehousing facility.

The Venture Organization

In the description of a venture analysis organization, a small cadre was recommended. As venture development is initiated, staffing must be designed to meet the objectives of precommercial activities. This staff of operational personnel should be as small as possible to carry out the tasks under an umbrella of enforced economy. However, false economies that do not provide for sufficient personnel with proper strengths to support the development should be avoided. Corrections in scope, talents, numbers, and disciplines can be made as modifications are required, always building a base for the commercial enterprise. A formal organization cannot always make normal distinctions between line and staff responsibilities. Flexibility is a byword, although it should not mask the need to prepare for a formal organization with distinct functional responsibilities when the venture is commercialized. The many ramifications of personnel requirements call for attention in the business strategy. Continual evaluation for the strongest organization will entail hiring, training, reorientation, and injection of supervisory talents.

People will supply the additional jobs in field service, technical service, and technical support. Where research missions are identified, some mechanism is needed to cope with this factor. During venture development, internal research is not advisable. Where some corporate support is available, the solution is obvious. Seeking outside contracts with industrial laboratories is a feasible route. Members of the field service, which might be defined as direct assistance to sales for such things as installation or demonstration, should be given priority. Technical service, which not only serves to respond, analyze, correct, and report on product problems, can be critical as well. Much depends upon the character of the product, and sales personnel might serve in these functions as part of their jobs. The salesmen should not be expected to make a lot of time-consuming service recalls. The important thing is to learn from the field experience, and learning about performance and application is closely allied to the merchandising approach used for the venture product.

Finances

Financial strategy is an integral part of the business strategy refined during venture development. It entails one of those collating operations that pervade New Venture Methodology. Piecing together the diverse segments into an integrated business would be meaningless without financial interpretation. Venture development provides the opportunity to refine the elements of costs, investments, sales projections, and the various yardsticks of financial reporting. It is imperative to pay early attention to the formal financial reports that will guide the venture management during development and commercialization and inform the corporate management. Writing an abundance of reports appears to be a burden, but when they are viewed as tools for monitoring and giving direction they can become accepted as routine. The commercial phase will require strict attention to fiscal matters, and during development, usable, informative, compatible formats can be set up on the basis of the individualized characteristics of the venture. Frequent and flexible economic reports set a pattern and reflect the true progress and outline of the business. These updated reports, in current use, become a part of the business strategy.

Business Proposal

There are other considerations as the strategy evolves into a formal business proposal. These have various implications and may relate to previously mentioned categories, but more often they overlap other disciplines or involve company policy and philosophy. For example, when a strategy is being developed, confidence in the future may be rising and falling as development results vary. Some question about the degree of risk may arise. If the pattern is unclear, a decision regarding the size of the production facility and its capacity may have to be made. Is a small-scale plant with room for expansion a better alternative than committing to a full-scale operation? Large costs are usually not saved by decreasing the initial plant capacity, and incremental investments for expansion can be so great as to overwhelm the hedge against failure. Is growth really planned? Can a transition be quickly made through rapid expansion?

At this juncture, judgment derived from experience in the development phase grossly affects the decision. It would be foolhardy to recommend one course of action over another. If it truly is a philosophic problem, the direction is clear. Either a good business opportunity exists or it does not. Where it does show viability, one can move with the confidence the venture has afforded. If it is questionable, commercialization might be delayed, reexamined, or rejected. With investment monies so critical and limited, they should not be diverted into poor prospects. Infusion of efforts into a lesser business opportunity denies and subverts New Venture Methodology. Perhaps it is logical to reassess the goals and objectives. When the original goals are shown to be inappropriate and the venture would survive under different circumstances, they can be restated. This kind of change is not necessarily bad.

When new goals become apparent, a special judgment is required concerning the preliminary data and the analysis on which these are based. The reassessment and subsequent reorientation may not be due to erroneous data but to a lack of pertinent data. In that case a decision must be made about reanalysis concurrent with continuation of the development. If confidence is high and the alteration is obviously not major or detrimental on the surface, such concurrent efforts are acceptable. Reanalysis will require full-time assignment of an analyst who is not involved in daily development activities. He becomes a venturer within the venture and retains the individuality and unidirectionality so important to obtaining a critical answer. This is permitted only when the assumption is made that results will be positive. However, if there is a chance the projected conclusions will be negative; if chance for success is reduced drastically; or if size of opportunity, degree of penetration, or financial goals are significantly less than anticipated, valid doubts arise about continuing the development.

Even when the results generate optimism, the effects of changing projected values should be viewed seriously. A temporary halt in development may not be feasible, or it may be a logistic impossibility. This only makes the decision to reject the venture more dramatic. It would be at worst foolhardy and at best naïve to allow a development to continue if it represents a poor risk or a misguided objective for the company. Analyses can be accelerated through intensive efforts and concentration of personnel. Many tasks take a finite time and more people don't help. This is not so with a review and reworking of the analyses. Therefore, a slowdown in venture development activities, assigning each person excused from operational duties a portion of the analysis, with all of them under the direction of the venture manager, would be the only viable alternative. The ability to make aggressive moves and decisions under duress is part of New Venture Methodology. The contribution of an early negative response after a reassessment is made results in major cost savings and less pain, especially if commercialization is begun at the wrong time.

Sales Volume

Other factors present themselves during venture development, including the recognition of the economies of size, the benefit of forward integration, the supplies of raw materials, and the synergistic effect of using existing talents and capabilities. Economies attributed to larger size and volume are not as true as is so often implied. There are certain things to look for in evaluating the large-volume sales problem. The large-volume buyer may require substantially better price breaks than originally assumed. It may mean additional costs to the seller owing to special handling, inventory, or distributional considerations. Selling a larger volume may produce better manufacturing margins, but it could burden sales effort, cash requirements, delivery systems, technical service, and other functions not apparent before the agreement to consummate the large sales order. The implications of a large order should be understood during the development phase, even if none is actually placed.

Forward integration was discussed previously as one method for securing a venture opportunity. Within a new venture, the same kind of approach might be appropriate. Experience in the field may indicate that the market need is greater than one the particular venture has chosen to solve. For example, a disinfectant for surgical washes might easily uncover a need for antiseptics in a variety of fields. Another example is the slow acceptance of a new raw material when its promotion is left to other converters. The greatest profit potential may also be available in upgrading the material. The venture may undertake the task. Service as part of the product package may loom as the better way to move. These cases illustrate the optimization or expansion of the venture opportunity and are not being used as tools to excuse poor performance or to revive a failing venture. It may be that forward integration becomes part of a long-range plan after commercialization because venture development has provided this guidance early in the business prognosis.

The matter of raw materials supply will also come under scrutiny during venture development. Sources of a construction material might be too limited, despite promises by a potential supplier. The supplier may not be venture oriented and might have accepted an obligation he cannot meet. On the other hand, numerous suppliers may come forward with claims of superior properties, better prices, and other tempting offers. The venture group must evaluate them. Frequently, differences in quality of feed stock occur, and these too must be understood in order to protect the quality of the product to be sold by the venture.

While backward integration is a plausible route for the future, any dependence upon it to make the venture grow is not recommended. If survival depends on developing a basic supply of components or raw materials, the venture is in jeopardy from the start. Then a reassessment problem arises because the objectives and goals are substantially changed. The same thinking applies to internal business synergisms. If synergisms exist or develop as a result of venture activity, they can be a plus. It is incumbent upon the venture staff to recognize and take advantage of them. They should be accepted as a benefit to the corporation, but not a necessity to venture development. Upon commercialization, the business strategy must take this into account for its fullest contribution and impact. Reliance upon a departmental or divisional synergism should not be part of the development phase, but must be considered in the strategy for commercialization.

Staff Functions

As development activities grow, many new questions arise. Some of these must be answered in order for a good business strategy to be proposed. Assistance from staff functions should not be overlooked. Where staff people are available, their skills should be used to the utmost. Although a venture is designed to be multidisciplinary with little or no dependence on outside groups, the venture development risk group must take a different approach. It cannot afford the luxury of self-contained specialists to do jobs in which staff people excel. The venture leader will seek support as he needs it and recommend that continuing needs be filled after commercialization.

Equally important are consultants, who may be specialists in the product area of operation, business generalists, technical advisers, or other experts. A great deal of assistance can be obtained this way without the permanent commitments of hiring new people to do the jobs. Administrative assistance can also support the venture. Where a personnel department is available, it can help to identify candidates and prepare official position descriptions, among other requisite forms. Legal and fiscal aid from the corporate umbrella can be used. The mature guidance of the administrative head to whom the venture leader reports cannot be overlooked, since, in part, his imagination and foresightedness had forged the institution of a venture approach, or at least created the right climate for it.

Reporting is integral to any business, and the time to set the pattern is during venture development. A lucid technique, suitable for the present and future and compatible with corporate needs, is required. While some kinds of reporting may be burdensome, they are necessary for control and monitoring by management. If the venture is to become a business, it must begin to function, at least within its own internal boundaries, like the excellent, self-sufficient business it will become. Exposure to the reporting process and experience from it may not become part of the strategy or proposal for commercialization, but they cannot be discounted in their value for convincing management that further appropriations are justified. While over-reporting implies a degree of overexposure, this need not occur. Reporting from the venture group to management can be concise and limited, while it can be thorough, detailed, and demanding for use within the group by the venture leader.

Unexpected Opportunities

Sometimes during venture development, though not often enough, new routes appear unexpectedly and it is important to be prepared for them. No amount of planning will prepare you to act, but if you remain flexible and alert, with a willingness to respond positively though not precipitately, you can quickly develop a plan. An ancillary opportunity might offer new and allied products, an available technology or license, a spinoff, or a request to purchase, distribute, or license. The venture's entry into a market with a product or even a product line may be too narrow. When the sales effort begins, customers dissatisfied with present competitive products may request others from the venture. Their insistence must be tempered by reality, though additional products may readily fit the venture plans. Caution should be exercised in expanding too early. It may be more apropos to delay expansion until later according to the business strategy. Efforts may be diluted in making a response without sufficient depth to support it.

Also, it may not be economical to expand at that particular time, so feasibility has to be surveyed as well. When success hinges on such expansion, it is advisable to return to the matter of reassessment of goals and objectives. Where it is expeditious and helpful and facilitates earlier achievement of checkpoints, reassessment needs serious consideration. The same may apply to an opportunity to purchase or license a compatible technology. In this case, the pressure is to make a commitment on the basis of the potential value. There is no need to act upon it immediately. Therefore, if a case can be made to move in the near future and still affect the venture positively, an option can be obtained or an agreement postponing any specific commitment can be made. Whereas any adverse effects on the venture would be minimal in acquiring new technology or making licensing arrangements, the effect on management is less attractive. Additional funds for the venture at this time might be viewed with a jaundiced eye. It takes an imaginative, aggressive, and committed management to act on the spur of the moment. If it takes too long to convince management the move is required, it can only be justified if the long-term result is substantial. Assignment of a full-time individual to put the proposal together will expedite its completion and acceptance and produce a better job.

Available spinoffs are another story. Ventures should be built on the basis of their ability to stand alone. Where acquisition of supportive assets is a requirement, there is significantly less chance of success. Reasons for this include such problems as a high price for the proper acquisition where excessive price-to-earnings ratios may be involved, unavailability of good buys, inheritance of traditional problems, and, of course, governmental regulations and existing laws. Any spinoffs considered here would be those that enhance the venture and are not necessary for the venture to succeed. The supplemental effect can be quicker commercialization at a lower cost, an influx of trained personnel, and shrinkage of the time scale in which to achieve venture objectives. As long as the purchased spinoff is small relative to the long-range venture size, there should be no question as to the advisability to proceed. Like any purchase, it must meet the business criteria. If and when it does and the purchase is complete, a new game begins. Venture development ceases and venture commercialization is entered.

The development phase becomes part of an ongoing business that must be given the priority it deserves. The venture leader is now a commercial manager and inherits the mantle. He must quickly reorganize to meet the challenge and adapt the risk group to support of the new business. While this has all the romance of an exciting adventure, it does subvert certain venture procedures. It is better, time allowing, to plan for such an acquisition as part of the business strategy after commercialization. This may not be possible since the available spinoff might be purchased by someone else or taken off the market. Long and complex discussions of acquisitions are not relevant to this text, but whenever possible, acquisitions should be incorporated into the company using high-quality business practices similar to those advocated in New Venture Methodology.

What about selling a venture during the development phase? Why not? To sell the venture indicates that it was basically in opposition to corporate objectives. If the objectives are to develop and sell businesses, this approach is acceptable. But where ventures are designed to promote growth of sales, profits, and returns, their sale negates these objectives. Of course, if a mistake is made, admitting it and saving or recovering losses by sale of the venture is no insult or sign of failure. But it remains a negative act and should always be interpreted that way. Licensing some portion of one's capability raises questions whose answers would be specific for the situation. Obviously, where licensing enhances the business (and this is not too readily seen), it should be carried out. Where it diverts, dilutes, or alters the direction, hence changes the goals, it is not recommended. Perhaps in the long range it should be considered within the context of the business strategy.

Distribution by a client or a manufacturer's representative is a different proposition. The best way to deal with it is to marginally commit to this procedure during development to see how it works. A short-term arrangement gives both parties a chance to evaluate their respective positions. When it is obviously part of the sales strategy rather than the general business strategy, the question remains moot and agreements should be processed on a short-term basis. Such agreements must be written with protections and flexibilities so that the venture does not rely entirely on the outside force or internal control evaporates. Again, this should be examined during the venture development phase and can become part of the resulting business strategy.

Ready for Commercialization

The finale of venture development is (1) a complete, well-documented business strategy, (2) from which a proposal to go commercial is derived, (3) for which funds are then appropriated. These are, in practice, three sequential steps. The business strategy is the culmination of the extended venture development phase. It describes the state and direction of the commercial venture. It covers that multitude of considerations described in this chapter as well as verification of the previous analyses. It is the beginning, not the end, and the venture embarks on a business journey as well planned and well defined as possible.

Any ventures adhering to New Venture Methodology that reach this stage are as close to no-risk as one can reasonably get. The business plan, like the aforementioned venture proposal, is the document used to convince and inform management to proceed and supply the required funds. Funds are ultimately the tools to carry out the plans and run the business. The business plan, which is a second proposal, distinguishing it from the venture proposal to form a risk group and enter the venture development phase, should contain certain elements.

- Summary—A brief description of the funds required, the business being started, the key factors, and the crucial elements.
- Background—An introductory statement including history, results, the opportunity, and objectives.
- Organization—An identification of key personnel, staffing requirements, structure, growth, and costs.
- Product—A reiteration of the product, product line, or service in all its ramifications, including its virtues and the need for it in the marketplace.
- Market—A description of the market, including its ultimate size available to the venture and a penetration rate, along with attention to external forces such as competition.
- Marketing—A sales strategy with emphasis on schedules, approach, people, customers, and distribution.
- Manufacturing—Facilities, their costs, capacity, margins, quality control, and key features of process and operation.
- Financial—Investment and other economic details presented in a clear, concise form with preliminary budgets for an initial period.
- Technical service—Support in terms of customer service, engineering, research, and product improvement.

This is the summation of intense preliminary efforts spanning a one- to two-year period. The achievement of these goals is no mean task. It should not be taken lightly since it is asking for a decision from management of major proportions. Investment dollars of serious magnitude will be involved. Commitment to a large and growing organization will be made. This, based on the business strategy evolved during the venture development stage, is the fundamental goal of New Venture Methodology.

The Venture Commercialization

To many entrepreneurs, venturing ends when commercialization begins. There are few arguments to refute or support such a belief. Within each phase of business development, concepts have been learned, experienced, modified, and reapplied within the format called New Venture Methodology. The impact of systematic approaches in the initial stage and especially in the analysis phase is great. The basis of New Venture Methodology is a strong foundation upon which the ultimate business will be built. In venture development, the capability to act unidirectionally and independently has many advantages. Rapid action made possible by intense planning, concise and painstaking decision making, small size, conservation of funds, and the presence of multidisciplinary capabilities during venture development are all factors for entrepreneurial action. A venture using these criteria has the benefit under the shelter of a large company that allows small, new businesses to arise and proceed rapidly in their early stages. Venture development is the intermediary step providing exposure and experience to confirm the analytical studies that lead to the proposal for a new business opportunity. The business strategy allows management to preview the detailed technique that will be used when monies are committed for commercialization. Venture commercialization can be accepted as a typical business function, perhaps mundane, but certainly well defined by an abundance of literature and a wealth of successful experiences.

New Venture Methodology does not take issue with the success American business has had surviving and growing in the marketplace, but it expands on this premise, especially in the initial steps. In venture commercialization a systematic and pragmatic method again appears as the single best way to commence and operate a successful business. Using all the modern tools available can be cumbersome and so time consuming that the business suffers. It is so much easier to neglect the use of all or any of them, or to utilize only the most obvious, rather than burden a manager with the task of studying and selecting the pertinent ones.

The translation of planning and reporting forms and monitoring documents into a proper, usable, and meaningful format may appear to be beyond the scope of the manager, and he settles for as few of them as his management absolutely requires. This is a narrow view and falls short of the goals set by New Venture Methodology. What is needed is a sufficient number of informative procedures for succinctly and candidly reporting and monitoring the business. These tools of management are used to recognize when new external forces are influencing the operation of the commercial enterprise. When early recognition of problems or changes occurs, decision response is rapid, and the action taken to allow for the new effect avoids adverse consequences. If the business flow is continuously jolted owing to late, after-the-fact occurrences, the result is sometimes chaotic, often confusing, and always detrimental. Periodic reporting by all segments of the new business sets a precedent of care and attention and allows individual prediction on the basis of readily apparent trends.

For these reasons, among many favoring the patterned approach in commercial developments, it is strongly recommended that as many critical reporting procedures be used as possible, avoiding the routine. Any routine business procedure in the area of control becomes extraneous. It is either ignored, irrelevant, or underused, all of which would indicate that the purpose for which the operation was originally developed has been eliminated or subverted. Any tools that are not fully used should be dropped or altered. Substitution of useful for bureaucratic procedures pays the dividend of keeping the venture leader on top of the business. Some of the tools in venture commercialization are the same ones that are integral to venture development. Others are incorporated in following discussions.

Before taking up the detailed points, some general review on the subject of tools might be helpful. The business strategy will delineate many segments of business necessary for effective and efficient commercialization. A reiteration of these as venture commercialization begins is most valuable. The separate steps of a programmed approach build successively on one another. The procedures designed and discussed in this text represent the thrust of New Venture Methodology and the dynamic result is a lower-risk, better-operating business. A final review of the product and its market outlined in the business strategy is important.

What subsegments are sought, and at what point in the business cycle? If there has been a change in demographics affecting consumption, responsive changes should be contemplated. Competition may also recognize the same opportunity as you did and its reactions are of prime concern. It is necessary to understand the possibilities that the product, customer, and market can change even as full-scale production is getting under way. The vagaries of the market can be pinpointed once the direct, open position of venture commercialization is taken. Analysis of trends is confirmed as the product-supply situation grows and aggressive sales action is taking place. The old relationships nurtured under venture development and the following ones born in expansion must be compatible. Customers are sensitive to the choice of other customers and expect equitable treatment. The need to adjust to the multiple pressures of sales, customer problems, and profits cannot be understated.

Basically a new set of criteria, developed from the new objectives under venture commercialization, is philosophically different from those derived during development stages. An example of this type of alteration is reexamination of the product's attributes. Although an earlier study may have been comprehensive, distinctive aspects may be discovered at any time in an operating business. New customers yield identifiably different needs or attributes. This is the basis for the well-known adjectives on consumer products such as *new, all new, new improved,* and the like, labels and size variations such as *family size, giant, de luxe, super,* and so forth. Products are thus positioned in view of market needs to help improve the potential for increased success. In addition, new value can result from customer acceptance. Though functional benefits were identified, they might not have been fully documented. Their actual value may have been understated. When customers compliment certain features, exploit them and capitalize on them. The converse is also true—that new knowledge can reorient customers' thinking and culminate in a series of redefinitions that remove some of the presupposed value-added components. Pricing can be reevaluated to respond to information gained from broader exposure. Production volume may need to be scaled to function economically in the altered environment.

Along the same lines, functionality, utility, or end use may change as a result of external contacts. An imaginative customer can discover a usage not suggested by your studies. A new set of circumstances might identify broader parameters for the product with a perspective for its function beyond that initially conceived. These contiguous opportunities may reorder the market approach. Because increased market exposure introduces functionality and opportunity not previously foreseen, flexibility to build in a new area is required during venture commercialization.

This flexibility must also allow for an expanded scale on the amount of advertising required. The kinds of ideas and the techniques used to help build sales rapidly could easily take more dollars than were projected. This means the product must be reviewed in regard to the advertising strategy and sales goals. What properties can get the attention of the buyer, can motivate user involvement, can incite or stimulate recognition of the product's uniqueness? The customer wants to be convinced, even though he knows his own problems and needs. To be supported in his view is beneficial to his attitude in favor of considering such a new product. This may be the stimulus for purchase. Whereas advertising was used sparingly during venture development, the pressure for increased sales dollars means that its importance grows. A position is needed to direct the customer to use the product or service to insure maximum growth of the commercial enterprise.

The business plan and its subplans growing out of the business strategy are to be implemented in the venture commercialization phase. Because these plans grow out of New Venture Methodology, they reflect the method in its many ramifications. As the major move is made into the marketplace, the plan will immediately come under new scrutiny. The market must be aligned to the forecast objectives in revenues. The field salesmen can identify users in terms of their potential volume consumption. The salesmen now begin the arduous task of specifying heavy users, medium users, and light users. They must determine the confidence they have in landing these accounts. Timing is critical so that manufacturing plans can be laid. Each market may need a separate and somewhat different strategy.

Sales Reports

The salesman has several reporting tools, among them the account report. It would contain typical information on the account, the call, and the required action. On each call he should fill out a form reflecting his activity and the customer's comments. Some follow-up action by him or someone else in the organization is needed to insure the proper attention to the customer's problems. By proper distribution of these reports, the entire commercial department can develop an overview. When the same complaints are repeated among homogeneous customer groups, the internal reaction system and tactics to deal with these consistent problem areas can be developed.

Another tool the salesman and his manager can use is the monthly sales report. It can include a customer list, the orders taken, projected orders, a call schedule, and a month-by-month or quarterly forecast. Figure 40 shows an example. This form allows for a quick accounting of the business relative to growth and future sales. A third document deals with invoices and new customers. These items can be handled separately or included on a single form. For example, as in Figure 41, a simple listing helps not only the salesman but his immediate management to evaluate the territory. It is a historical review and a plan combined, and doesn't need the time-consuming efforts required to make a lengthy strategy report. All these data can be kept up to date from the call reports, the order file, and technical service requests. The latter are necessary so that a technical-service group can respond to the salesman's needs and also record the product problem areas. Whereas these documents may seem excessive in their requirements

Figure 40. Sales report.

Date _____
Month, Year

Customer	Orders last year		Orders this year		Projected sales			Call schedule
	Units	Dollars	Units	Dollars	Next Month	Quarter	12-Month	

Figure 41. Sales status report.

Date _____
Month, Year

	Customer List	Orders	Invoices	Back-orders	Potential	Calls	Use/Product
Existing							
New							
Projected							

in a mature business, the subject here is a new commercial enterprise that is using a systematic technique to lower risk and insure success. Mature, complex businesses do, of course, use computer printouts to keep track of orders and invoices.

Manufacturing Considerations

Dealing with the product or service to be sold, certain considerations can be incorporated into venture thinking as it is reordered and adjusted to meet the volatile market. When the new commercial plant starts producing, unlimited quantities of goods are theoretically available. Where services are the product, supply is a function of the capability to build up a sufficiently large staff to accept all orders and contracts. However, theory and practice diverge, and volume productivity does not occur instantaneously. For this reason, product quotas and schedules must be set. The progression from a pilot operation to a small-lots operation to initial startup to full-capacity production determines the quantities of product available at specific times. Where there are other limiting factors such as raw material availability, it, too should be considered. This is a manufacturing consideration, but it can be related to sales as a factor controlling the availability of the product to customers. Other product-oriented policies include labeling, packaging, handling, and sampling where applicable. Pricing, a perspective discussed independently, is a hybrid of market, product, and production.

The manufacturing function will operate in three separate areas as well. It will be producing for sales from a small-scale production operation which has the additional objective to help design, build, and finally run the full-production operation. Production can be a very complex problem or a simple one, such as assembling purchased components. In any case, production supplies the data on product availability and its flow with time. Sales will adjust according to the ability to produce. Any commitment made along these lines should be taken extremely seriously, since it is a critical area. Late deliveries, poor product, and wrong product are intolerable to the customer and the sales force.

The manufacturing operation may also wish to reestablish guidelines for the process. Methods and procedures will be formalized in a policy manual for the actual plant facility. Previous efforts along these lines operated on the basis of different plant facilities, whose procedures can be used as guides in preparing new documents. New views on the location of facilities are probably not possible at this juncture, since site selection should have been completed in the business plan. However, review and cost evaluations made on the basis of the chosen site should be detailed and finalized. Local contacts within the social and business communities can be developed. These management problems are in addition to such critical aspects of manufacturing as materials balance, inventory control of both raw and finished goods, and a conclusive cost-accounting procedure.

This represents a relationship with financial considerations. The reporting of inventory levels on a monthly basis is a control for manufacturing and a guide for sales. Sales, in turn, would assist the production staff by informing them about seasonal or cyclic trends that the manufacturing operation must prepare for prior to any inordinate demand. Materials balance and labor input help to prepare a standard cost that fits the cost-accounting system. Cost accounting should be standardized, and it is helpful if expertise is supplied by the parent company. Where cost accounting is developed by the venture, a sophisticated accountant is required. There should not be a sterile bookkeeping procedure, but one that has meaning to the venture leader and his manufacturing manager since they must make many decisions on the basis of such data.

Technical Service

Technical service, one of the salesman's tools, is an asset when properly utilized. Since the need for technical service is usually great early in venture commercialization and diminishes with time, not only in dollar sales but absolutely, overstaffing can occur. It is far better to build a technical service group according to a plan with certain optimistic assumptions concerning product performance. Although we do not condone insufficient technical support when support is required, we do advocate efficient use and controlled scheduling to avoid its abuse. While the service staff works to correct customer complaints, both real and imagined, it should also be self-curing or self-eliminating by reporting back potential customer problems and recommended solutions before field complaints occur. Manufacturing and sales corrections should be immediate reactions to limit such field problems—the manufacturing function, by improving its techniques, and the sales staff, by selling only to approved and workable end uses. Technical service also aids in supporting public relations releases, publicity, sampling, literature claims, end-use techniques, and other selling appurtenances. Within the technical auspices, there should also be a product-development function. Whether this is part of a technical group servicing internal needs or part of an adjacent technical group must be decided by the venture leader with management's concurrence.

Personnel

Even though an organization has grown to maturity during venture development, changing needs may indicate that appropriate alterations should be made. Administrative functions are readily adjusted. The working and operational structures that took shape during the venture development phase are more or less fixed for some period of time. The organizational approach was formulated on the basis of actual experience and, barring individual or emotional assertions, it is best designed to introduce the planned business to the market. New personnel requirements are the most difficult and time consuming. Rather large increases in employees with certain manufacturing skills will be needed. The choice of people according to job descriptions and job procedures is not simple. To procure, train, and hold good people is a major production problem in and of itself. This will be an important part of the initial phase of venture commercialization. Some such matters do not evolve but are sudden and require intense attention. Needless to say, other negotiations involving personnel relations, including labor considerations, the professional staff, and supportive personnel will have to be dealt with at the outset. Dilettantes are not recommended for handling this, since specialists are more suited to such complicated tasks and personnel services do a precise and effective job.

An important factor to be considered here is the naming of the general manager. Up to this point, he has been referred to as the venture leader. If the original entrepreneur who found and nurtured the opportunity is chosen—and this is strongly recommended—then one set of guidelines can be used. He has been strongly committed and has developed the original dynamic financial planning documents. He knows the value of continual correcting and updating. No divergence from the plan would be expected when he goes commercial.

If another person is assigned as general manager—and without exception he should be totally responsible, fully committed, and assiduously guarded from any other tasks or objectives—he will retain the right to make adjustments in the business plan. Since he is inheriting someone else's calculations and decisions, his interpretation of the financial data may be sufficiently different to make it desirable for him to take a quick, fresh look at them. This recommendation, however liberal-sounding, does require an extremely strong argument to convince corporate managers to allow the new general manager to alter the financial basis of the venture commercialization. Their original approval was given on the basis of financial data supplied as an integral part of the venture proposal. Only strong and undeniable propositions would persuade them to accept such early variations. Two ways to avert this problem would be to make certain that the general manager, whoever is appointed, be part of the organization before commercialization, or that he accept, at least for the initial phases of commercialization, those financial projections he inherits. Time and performance will best prove the justification for modification as he monitors and reports progress on a regular basis.

Finance

Finance, the queen of the venture, has a part in all the previous discussion areas. How much will be spent on marketing? What does the product cost? What are our investment figures? Marketing is a budgeted expense and must be represented as a component of pricing. Advertising, which is a fixed cost, will be controlled on a product-sales basis as the business matures, but it can represent a disproportionate dollar cost in the initial phases of commercialization. These and other considerations are reviewed at all stages of a venture.

Data Collection

Since a venture is an implemented plan, flexible and dynamic, one is hard pressed to see how or where it could fail to produce a viable commercial business. It can fail if planning misses the mark in any of its several areas. The first and most important of these is the quality of the planning information. If the data are inadequate or unsuitable, catastrophe is possible. Unfortunately, internally generated data, without field support, are inadequate and unsuitable because they tend to rely on a common external source.

The venture leader's reliance on library studies that accept the most recent articles by an acknowledged specialist means that he, not the leader, is running the venture. The importance of breadth and depth of information audits cannot be overstressed, and many impeccable sources should be used without relying on only one acknowledged source. Another reason for failure of planning is the mistaken idea that strategic planning, especially as it relates to financial aspects, is synonymous with action planning. The extrapolative nature of strategy must be supplanted by the actual pragmatic plan that deals with day-to-day business. Projections are not eliminated, but they are included only for the near future and are limited to those needed for good and substantial operation of the business.

Still another mistake is failure to recognize written objectives. The majority of people rely on unstated objectives, or use such flexible ones that the plan is stifled. The objectives must not only be written, but used, restated, reaffirmed, and followed. If the objectives change, so must the plan. These must be compatible. However, the argument for objectives must never subvert implementation, and action should proceed on the basis of the most agreeable objectives possible at the time. This allows everyone to operate by a plan. All too frequently, the management philosophy is to look over and around the plan. The get-things-done attitude indicates that the plan inhibits business activity. This reflects former circumstances when hectic exercises in superfluous conversation, bitter argument, and frustration made planning an unpleasant experience. For plans to work, everyone must operate under them and the power of management should not circumvent them. When everyone has contributed, when a continuous, uninterrupted approach has been activated, and when plans are recognized as dynamic and not always achievable in their initial form, opportunity for business success is greatly improved. When the planners are the operators and plans are their tools, the chance of ultimate success is further magnified.

Timing

Choosing the right time to go commercial is a frequent concern. Because one is dealing with a continuum, no specific timing can be recommended for venture commercialization. It varies with the corporation as a sequential portion of the exploitation of a business opportunity. The best advice one can offer is that after an opportunity is selected it should be analyzed immediately. When results are positive, do not hesitate to set up a venture development effort. When it has proved successful, the byword is: Act now. The time to develop the business is now. This action determines what a company does now and will be doing next year. If the opportunity is there, move accordingly. Too often the decision is delayed until factors in the marketplace, attitudes of the corporate managers, or certain interests and commitments among the risk group invalidate the assumptions and render the situation too far gone for successful action. Where the facts are in hand and corporate yardsticks are an inherent part of the objective, the venture commercialization should be initiated.

The arbitrary use of measurements within the venture development phase can serve as a key justification. A certain sales volume, a change in cash flow, an ROI level are all possible checkpoints from which to proceed to market. Unfortunately there are as many negative as positive features in using them. However, the one- or two-year limit on venture development, coupled with these other factors, is a good basis for a balanced decision to go commercial. Whatever happens, consistency in following the plan, in the people involved, and in the performance of the product and the market are areas to emphasize. Another matter to handle carefully is delegation of authority, the measure of a true manager. The more intrusive he is and the more he is involved in routine execution, the less ready he is to lead.

All the factors to consider cannot be anticipated here, since they are specific to particular situations. But decision points, predetermined on the basis of consistent appraisal limits or goals, are necessary. Remember that early, decisive action grounded in sound information and plans gives a business opportunity the best chance to become a commercial success. Don't get trapped in inaction only to see competitors grow and flourish in a business you identified years earlier.

Pricing

Prices must be soundly and precisely assigned to the product as a result of the best available data from the marketplace. During venture development, much data have been accumulated. However, the volatility of the market increases the opportunity for error. It is fickle and responds to the slightest stimulus. Too high a price and you founder, too low and you go broke. The buyer's only measure is value-in-use. This is not always a profitable price, or it may vary so widely for each customer it evades the best technique for analysis. The company or the venture bases its price on its criteria of costs. Product cost, cost of sales, ancillary costs, and profit are added to compute the necessary price. The time element enters the picture, since it determines the volume at which the projected costs are attained.

Other considerations in setting the price for an item include the market and social and psychological factors. When a proprietary position is held, a specific need fulfilled, a new unopposed entry made, or there is a product shortage in relation to demand, the pricing decision is less sensitive to error in judgment. The social aspects are, of course, related to the type of user. When someone of high social status uses a product, it often catches on and becomes popular. In industry, products and techniques also find greater acceptance when leaders use them. Name-brand distilled spirits are highly susceptible to this sort of influence. The absence of intensive television and radio advertising seems to be easily overcome by a mysterious grapevine that elevates one brand, then another, to rather prestigious levels. It becomes the social brand of the moment. Consider in addition to this the market psychology, and it becomes more and more difficult to understand the unpredictable buyer. He often buys for unexplainable reasons, and pays the price for an estimate he makes devoid of fact, logic, and reason.

One could easily relate many varied effects on pricing that enter into the pricing decision. These are criteria that depend on the product, market, company, or situational characteristics and influence the movement of price up or down. For example, in markets with short product lives because of technology, such as the electronics and drug industries, higher prices are justified owing to the high initial dollar input and short life cycle. This is not categorical, and should be evaluated on an individual price basis. Sales volume is important, since it can justify a lower price owing to greater efficiencies in production. This is not always true when there is a high labor input. The more automated the process, the lower the potential price level can be. Competition, limited variations on the product line or mix, and the stage of growth or age of the operation influence price. Geographics, the number of customers, technical service, and the dollar-per-item ratio may also account for variations in pricing considerations. The final or ultimate user, the number of people in the distribution channel, and the need for inventory at all levels will contribute to the pricing decision. Pricing should be fixed during commercialization to (1) achieve sale goals, (2) sustain growth, (3) balance sales and production, (4) adjust within markets, and (5) achieve profit goals.

Success as a Goal

The entire objective of a venture is to achieve success in the marketplace. What has the best opportunity for success? A venture that has the basic characteristics of success built in during the early stages. There is, however, no guarantee of business success. The sudden influx of new management people, line employees, larger facilities, and increased capital, both fixed and working, introduce new complexities.

The venture should have a profile that answers the following requirements of the venture staff. Do the leader and his key personnel have the proper expertise? They should be aware of the industry they are operating in, have developed experience and sensitivity to the technology and the market, and recognize the position their product will occupy in the market. They must be highly motivated and self-starting. Many sacrifices are often necessary during the early stages. Devotion to the unidirectional program can alter the working hours of committed individuals. They are called upon, through personal motivation, to give up free time, extracurricular pleasures, and often the simple amenities of life to support the incipient commercial success.

Another important quality is leadership. Complete accountability does not excuse failure to delegate responsibility, which we reemphasize because it is so important. The general manager must not only speak out forcefully for his view, but for the composite view of his personnel. He has to operate up and down with equal vision, commanding respect and attention in both directions. He must be able to induce talent to join the commercial enterprise, and keep them during times of trial. He must also be able to see the venture commercialization through the formative period. To do these things he must have personal traits of the highest order. Can he admit errors, is he willing to back down, to accept facts? Integrity, decisiveness, orderliness, and a sense of deep loyalty are needed. The ideal entrepreneur is also open-minded, inventive, ingenious, quick, practical, and independent. Finally, he must be given autonomy and freedom of action in order to achieve success.

Success also can be a function of the product or project device. About 50 percent of new products introduced commercially effect market changes; hence the need for strong market capabilities. Approximately 50 percent require new, improved, or substantially modified manufacturing. This is reflected in the consistent demand for better attention to the production–manufacturing function while venturing. These numbers are not additive, and there is overlap. It is also known that 50 percent of new products taken to market cause overall business changes for the company, through marketing, manufacturing, and other operational portions of the organization. This indicates that only by purposeful generation of opportunities that can be handled without painful reorientation can the chance of success be increased.

Other data support systematic approaches. About 40 percent of successful new products result from systematic needs analyses, 30 percent from systematic product attribute analysis, 20 percent from general problem solving resulting in direct product or business opportunities on the basis of the solutions, and 10 percent from miscellaneous sources. Such data may be skewed from year to year and industry to industry, but they indicate the absolute requirement for systematic versus random approaches.

Many times, dollar support for a venture is minimal. This makes it necessary to choose low-cost and consequently smaller opportunities. To the giants, these are too insignificant, since a $10 million business has little impact on a billion-dollar corporation. Even large corporations sometimes seem unwilling to fund innovations. This reluctance has been discussed frequently by others, and may in fact exist. A lack of convincing evidence that a venture should be pursued may really be the reason, not a lack of commitment by corporate management. It can't logically turn down a well-planned and well-documented opportunity for substantial sales growth and profits. When smaller opportunities are undertaken, with less time and fewer personnel available, some of the important considerations will be given priority. Although all ideas presented to an analyst are considered and weighed, only a minimum are subjected to any formal screening. Those with minimum investment pass on the first screening. Process, services, techniques, and formulations are given precedence over products. Since people cost the most money, they are hired only when the need exists.

Technological equipment or small ventures are often purchased when the internal competence does not exist. Whereas purchasing the opportunity appears to be the easiest alternative, it almost always has the highest risk and is the most expensive and least desirable method. Internally generated and home-grown opportunities are best, for both small and large corporations. When opportunities come from outside, large corporations will uniformly find that unless they are significant in size at the outset, perhaps $5 million to $10 million in sales with a proprietary or unique position, no profit progress will result. Small companies are cautioned to avoid ambitious, internal, large-size commitments. The converse is true for large companies. They should avoid the small, externally generated, conservative, and low-risk opportunities that don't move easily in a large corporate environment. They require a disproportionate time investment and result in no substantial benefit to the company.

Risk and Uncertainty

One cannot discuss success from new ventures without assessing the risk of the venture commercialization phase. Risk and uncertainty analyses are possible using a simulation model. Risk analysis is a technique whereby input variables, including specific uncertainties, are translated into performance characteristics. These measurements can be made as they affect performance and can be computed as profiles. Uncertainty is a probability function affecting the evaluation of financial variables. It differs from the optimistic/pessimistic/most-probable analysis, which makes assumptions that defy specific quantification. Sensitivity, the effect on one variable at a time, shows its effect on the outcome of the proposed and projected data, but it does not indicate the chance of such a deviation occurring. Using all these techniques improves one's understanding of the business, and when quantification is attempted, it forces certain modes of thinking related to external and/or internal influences. Details on the value of risk profiles, uncertainty profiles, and sensitivity can be found in several good references specifically dealing with them.

Pragmatically, the use of investment tools after the fact may be questionable, but they can be more meaningful if some historical input is available. The associated risks are real. They are not mathematical, and the less mathematical the technique, the more it will be used and understood. For a venture entering commercialization, the use of risk analysis is limited to determination of the venture's sensitivity to important forces. By that time, to use it to analyze a venture's acceptability to the company is a superfluous effort, although there is some virtue in comparing the venture with others, past, present, or future.

It is unfortunate that risk analysis cannot be easily applied to conceptual research projects to determine the best opportunity for success. The problem is choosing the right yardsticks for evaluating risk or performance. Dollar returns and those financial calculations that deal with profits as related to sales are frequently the guidelines set to measure risk. When the input for an analysis becomes specious, as it usually is early in the game, little meaning can be assigned to the results of risk analysis. Experience indicates that it can be done, and shows some statistical reliability. One wonders whether the gross judgments of an individual were really performing the tasks resulting in good choices, rather than the mathematical tool. Of course, only limited sampling is available for the type of experience referred to in this case.

If risk analysis is used at the start of venture commercialization, and it is recommended to do so, the significant factors to consider are sales, operating expenses, fixed and working capital, and pricing. The probability of achieving the indicated sales volume will change with the volume of anticipated sales. At low volume, probability is high that the anticipated sales will be reached. Supplying data on probability as a consequence of external and internal factors yields a curve that describes sales dollars with appropriate percentages of probability to achieve them. This can then be applied to a yardstick such as return on sales or investment. Other similar relationships can be developed for operating expenses, investment, or pricing. These can be translated to the probability of falling below chosen levels. In turn, each will reflect the probability of reaching the projected returns. This is done by asking suppositional questions. The meaning assigned to these relationships is most important. When projected sales goals are greatly affected by existing influences, chances of attaining the goals are diminished. The probability curve is steep, warning management about the risk involved. Perhaps more modest sales figures are then in order.

The influence of potential market competition should show only minor effects, although combined with several inputs it might again result in reassessment. The operating costs and investment dollars are controllable, and the probability curves indicate the degree of latitude one has in fixing and exercising that control. Pricing feeds back into the sales figures, though it is sufficiently important to be handled independently. Risk analysis avoids the pitfalls of classical statistics that use standard deviations, using more realistic, properly weighted assumptions to assess the risk and divergence from the projections. Here the deviations are real and specific for the individual case. Use of risk analysis with other business tools aids and improves understanding and decision making.

Risk Analysis

Risk analysis uses probability distributions for the various input variables. Values can then be selected randomly from each of these distributions and used in the appropriate evaluative formula. Repeated trials will produce a distribution of results, and each venture considered will yield a different distribution of final results. Final selection of worthwhile ventures can be made by evaluating each against the absolute criteria the company has set for new-venture selection and by selecting the best of those opportunities that surpass these absolute standards.

The probability distributions used in risk analysis are based on input supplied by the venture group members in closest contact with the facts. For example, sales are often the most difficult input to determine accurately. Estimated sales, however, are critical to assessing the commercial attractiveness of a venture. It is necessary, therefore, to estimate the probability of achieving certain sales levels; these estimates are provided by the marketing member of the venture group.

Figure 42 is a graph showing a result of such estimates. It shows that
as dollar sales increase, the probability of reaching these sales de-
creases. This might reflect the market analyst's view that at a low
level of sales there would be no competition. As sales increase, competitors might enter the field and a projected drop in price would be
likely. It is apparent that there is little doubt that low sales will be
achieved. But, as the dotted line indicates, there is a zero percent
probability of achieving $500,000 in sales or, conversely, there is a
100 percent chance that less than $500,000 in sales will occur. In
using these probabilities, we must recognize that these, too, are estimates. So we can superimpose an uncertainty profile on the estimate.
The uncertainty of estimates is shown in Figure 42 by the vertical

**Figure 42. Probability and uncertainty of achieving
projected sales levels.**

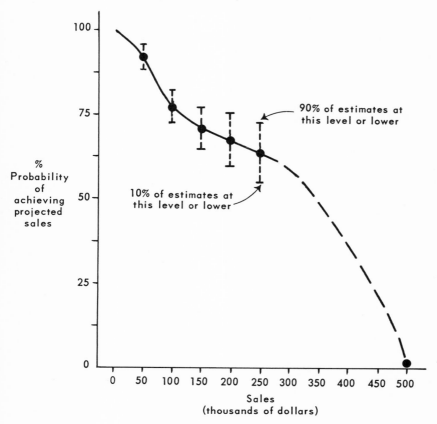

lines through each of the points. These lines represent the range
within which 80 percent of the estimates of the probability of achieving each level of sales would fall if such estimates were obtained from
a large number of judges. The central points represent the means of
these distributions. So, for example, the graph indicates that the mean
percentage probability of achieving sales of $250,000 is approximately
63.7 percent, but that 10 percent of the time the probability of achieving this level of sales would be 54.2 percent or smaller, and 10 percent of the time the probability of achieving it would be 70.8 percent
or larger. The length of each line indicates the extent of agreement
among the judges, short lines indicating substantial agreement, long
lines lesser agreement. In most operating situations, such distributions
would not usually be so symmetrical around the mean.

A problem that might be examined using risk analysis is a situation in which sales in units, price, manufacturing cost, and distribution costs vary within estimated ranges. For example, the variation

Figure 43. Probability for return on investment.

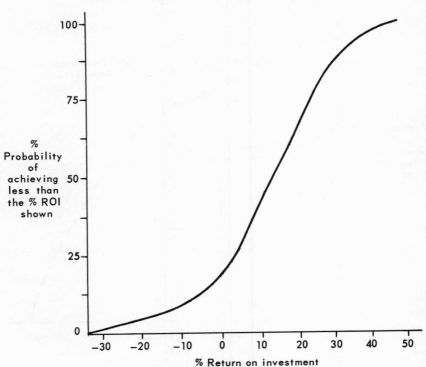

Figure 44. Comparison of venture ROIs.

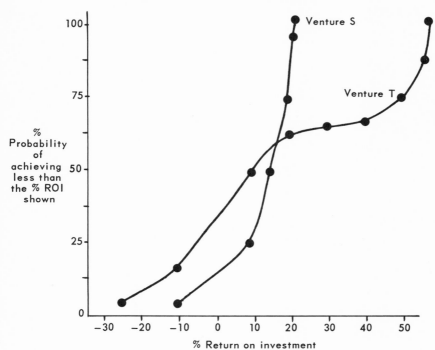

for units sold would be between 1,000 and 5,000, for price between $50 and $100 per item, and for potential cost for the production and sale of the product between $35 and $85 per item. Specific sets of values could be selected randomly and repeatedly from each of these distributions and put into a straightforward profit-per-unit formula. When units, profit per unit, and investment are taken together, a distribution of percentage return on investment could be prepared. If the venture passed the absolute hurdle to acceptance and was better than other available ventures, it might be selected for further development. Figure 43 presents a return on investment (ROI) distribution and demonstrates the relative confidence one can have in reaching a particular ROI. It shows that there is a 20 percent chance of getting less than 25 percent ROI or an 80 percent probability of achieving it. In addition, one can compare ROIs for two or more different ventures. The probabilistic nature of the ROIs can be demonstrated by using a curve showing the probability of reaching the desired ROIs. In Figure 44 Venture S shows less probability of producing less than a 10 percent ROI than Venture T, while Venture T has the greater chance to reach a 30–40 percent ROI. So, while they might be judged similar, the risk is shown to be somewhat higher for Venture T but the rewards are potentially greater.

Risk analysis techniques can also be applied to sales forecasts that extend over a number of years. Figure 45 indicates the kind of information that can be obtained to assist in decisions based on projections of future sales. It shows the relative chance of achieving the indicated sales for each of the years listed. The band of uncertainty for *year one* is small. However, as future years are examined, the band of uncertainty broadens. For each year, however, the median value is chosen for locating the curve, since it represents the most likely level of sales. The lack of symmetry of the bands indicates skewing of the uncertainty profiles; the closer the end of the uncer-

Figure 45. Uncertainty of projected sales volume.

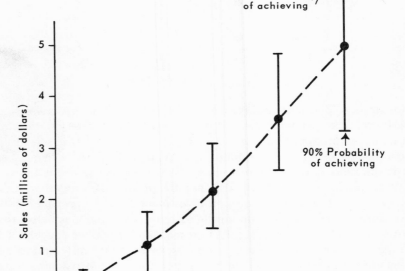

tainty band to the mean, the greater the concentration of sales estimates in that region.

Policies and Procedures

A commercial operation requires certain guidelines that can be overlooked during the volatile development stage. While learning does not stop, there is some need for standardization and stability, for manuals and written policies to direct the day-to-day operation. While ventures under a corporate umbrella can borrow or must adhere to the policies of the parent, it is often expeditious to design some slightly different or at least more specific ones for the venture. Documents dealing with process procedures and job descriptions will be modified according to the actual plant operations or the jobs performed within the business. However, there are matters related to daily practices that need attention. Policies on holidays, vacations, sick leave, and working hours need formalization. Employee relations get first priority, since people and their attitudes make or break the commercial enterprise. Safety manuals, security procedures, telephone usage, petty cash, and the like all require some written guidance. It is not the intention here to draw up such a list, but only to remind the general manager of his obligation. A typical index to assist in preparing a policy manual will be found in the Appendix. Most corporations have all these areas covered within central policy manuals. Where decentralization is the practice, organized divisions have such manuals that can serve as a model for the new business personnel policy. It is important, since undesirable practices are difficult to correct and habits are not easily broken after they are ignored for any operational period of time.

Growth

If one is to justify venturing with New Venture Methodology, it must be brought to commercialization. The object of achieving such a goal must be growth—profitable growth of the company with corresponding growth of its people. This universal goal among management executives is nurtured, lauded, discussed, surveyed, and acted upon in every way conceivable. However, there are only a limited number of ways to grow: expanding sales in present market areas, holding a percentage penetration while demand grows, penetrating a new market area with old products, introducing new products, creating new markets, and consummating mergers and acquisitions. The difficulty in expanding sales in present markets, requiring a battle with competition and increased expenditure in sales aid or some type of incentives, is that it is too frequently short-lived and not sufficiently productive. The easy way, and that most accepted by industry during periods of healthy economic growth, is to hold one's own and grow with demand. This is the mode of growth that all industry counts on. The end of its practice is not now in sight, and it will continue to be a substantial part of the thinking of many industries not plagued with overmature product life cycles and tremendous competition. New products designed to fill unmet needs actually fit in the new-market area. New markets with old products will, again, be handled divisionally, except where a market so foreign as to be outside the scope of present business capabilities is being sought. Here venture selection, analysis, and development is recommended highly.

The single best opportunity for growth that is consistent with New Venture Methodology is in the creation of new markets. Because the failure of business entries has time after time been caused by marketing shortcomings, venture methods provide a sound mechanism for curing this ill. Flexibility and autonomy with unidirectionality and multidisciplinary characteristics give New Venture Methodology the added muscle to succeed where marginal success or outright failure has predominated. It is no panacea, but judiciously followed, it does mitigate the high probability of failure. Mergers and acquisitions are growth routes whose value is measured by the annual-report income statements. This growth is instantaneous, and with revitalization or new parent infusions, there can be continuing growth. It is a financial investment with some very fixed and definable parameters. As a venture route, it deserves no more than passing mention except to say that any new addition can be integrated more easily by instituting venture-type reporting and monitoring. Ventures of this sort have proven generally unsatisfactory, with the usual number of exceptions. This is not to say they were poor investments, but they may have been below par.

Personnel

The growth of the people in the venture organization is probably the single most important facet of venturing. The aggressive, talented people assigned to a venture or who have chosen venture management as a career are the best source for future corporate management. Their education in business operations is not only intensive, they will have covered all business disciplines within a time scale compressed up to three times that of ordinary operations. Because of the extreme and diverse effort key members of a venture expend, the one year of actual time spent yielding three years' worth of experience can be demonstrated if not absolutely proved. Studies refer not only to the gray hairs of venture leaders and groups, but to the accumulation of knowledge and the spirit of decision making. Rewards should reflect this, although a discussion of compensation is avoided under New Venture Methodology. Rewards are not part of the method, but are rather a sign of enlightened management.

More important than providing compensation is to avoid stifling the people. The signs of inhibition are unmistakable. Talented young people leave the company after short periods of employment. Prospective talent turns down offers of employment. Fired-up employees start to taper off and become almost nonproductive. The flow of ideas ceases, which usually becomes apparent when no one wants to take on any additional ventures. An avocation becomes a person's central concern, extracurricular activities are accelerated, work hours are rigidly adhered to, and a general malaise sets in. It is the exceptional man who continues to perform despite the lack of support and interest from management. His motivation is usually internal, and he will succeed somewhere else if he is not allowed to do so in his present situation. On the other hand, pride, activity, satisfaction, contribution, and sacrifice are apparent among those properly compensated and visibly growing in the organization. It is the obligation of management to accept new ventures enthusiastically if it embarks on a venture program. The people need it for growth. Without personal growth, corporate growth ceases. When ventures are working, they should be nutritiously fed. Venturing does work, and where it has, the net result has been corporate growth of the first magnitude.

10

The Maturation

IN time, a commercial enterprise reaches a point at which the dynamics of the market and the role of the product or service cease to allow further growth. While growth may not slow to zero, it becomes substantially less than normal expansion owing to national factors. This is the mature phase of the business. In the definition assigned to maturation as a continuous process within the context of New Venture Methodology, it begins much earlier.

In fact, the gradual transition that takes place in the venture commercialization phase from market development to market maintenance is often insidious. A maturation phase is suddenly noticed by all although it has already begun before the signs are apparent. It may be important to plan initially to stimulate the growth vitality by constant infusions of new products, processes, services, or techniques. But this is not the function of a venture group. The necessity for operating organizations to insure internal growth in areas that relate to or are compatible with existing business has been stressed. Maturation from the venture standpoint is that point at which the need for rapid change and strict adherence to a single goal has moderated. It is the decision time at which management must assess the commercial operation. Then an additional decision concerning its fate must immediately follow. To allow the new business to float, without direction, guidance, and future disposition, is a poor move. The periodic review of the business should have indicated some better course of action. An early decision is required with specific attention to this detail to maintain a smooth operation and secure the commitment of the operating personnel. The alternatives are discussed in this chapter, as they are affected by the source of the venture, the type of business and its character, and the financial state it has achieved.

Divisional Inheritance

The source of the venture is important when the disposition is considered because, by implication, it affects the decision. If the venture opportunity was suggested or initiated by internal sources, their participation in the decision is implicit. Their influence cannot be minimized. Often they champion an opportunity they present for the venture commitment, and sometimes they have ulterior motives for supporting their candidate. If a division cannot handle a particular opportunity but finds it most interesting, the management might suggest a venture approach because it is good for the division as a source of new growth, which in turn is good for the company. In small companies, this should present no difficulty. In the larger corporation, divisional squatter's rights or at least a first rejection can enshroud the entire program. Where the reasons for a clear-cut decision to award a maturing commercial enterprise to a certain division are obvious, no problems occur. If two or more divisions are competing, the problem increases in complexity. When the source of the venture recommendation is not divisional, no division may feel the venture fits, or is willing to include it within its profit center. This should seldom happen since the business will have been proved a growth opportunity, increasing sales and expanding profits, which is beneficial to the division.

Business Character

Staff Sources
Sometimes the idea for a venture project comes from a venture group or corporate staff group, such as a research and development team, engineering department, planning group, or market research staff. If the venture group was originally responsible for the selection, the way is clear for them to recommend the best administrative home for the mature enterprise. When the research and development staff is involved, there can be a problem regarding the source of funds and final disposition of the new business. If the work, and hence the potential opportunity, emanates from programs corporately funded, management is free to determine where the venture will be placed. If the

project was divisionally funded, the source must be considered, which, for practical purposes, is the funding division. When other staff groups are involved, each may determine some particular avenue to be the best route for the venture. If they adhere to their beliefs, the impact of their recommendations will necessarily be felt at the time the decision is made and the conflict will have to be resolved.

External Sources

External sources of the venture opportunity present a more complex problem. When a license or other physical portions of a business must be acquired, the management makes certain assumptions about the future home of the venture at the time of purchase or agreement. Unless new, strong forces change the attitude, these initial directions will prevail—and well they should if the plan was based on those assumptions. If an external source was the originator of the opportunity but it was discovered through the venture search, screening, and selection process, the tendency is to consider it an internal development. This is especially true if no external payment to a consultant or finding service is made. The source can affect the disposition, and a pragmatic manager recognizes this throughout the business development stages.

Type of Business

Of equal importance to the decision on disposition of the new business is the type of business and its character. The venture-turned-commercial-enterprise can be quite diverse in its market approach and its relative position to the basic projections. Whether a business offers a product or service can grossly influence where it should be housed. Small businesses are less attractive to divisional profit centers, whereas larger ones may be capable of standing on their own as independent entities. The same applies if the business is apparently highly successful or only marginally so. A healthy profit center would be reluctant to inherit a marginal performer. If the profit center is marginal or in some trouble, it would be more amenable to taking the venture business. Alternately, if the high success of a venture can be capitalized on, there may be some hesitation to associate it with any other profit center for the duration of its maximum growth period, especially if the profit center is a poor one.

Another matter to consider is the venture's match with other internal enterprises. Where a good match is obvious or economies can be realized by combining the new business with an existing one, the decision is simpler. Synergism is often presented as an argument in favor of combination, but it should be carefully analyzed, since skepticism raises the question of whether synergism actually exists in these cases or is possible. A judicious search should substantiate or negate this claim.

Still another aspect of the character of the new business is its staff. When the venture business is highly structured and fully staffed, it can be more or less attractive depending upon the viewpoint of the adopting division. Its benefit is that no additional personnel need be hired or transferred from other positions. Negatively, it may appear overstaffed, presenting an unusual expense burden to the divisional operating unit. Further, there is no convenient way to incorporate middle management from the adopting division to influence and direct the new business along lines more acceptable to its present procedures. Perhaps this is an advantage, but it tends to be a problem to most managers. If a lean staff or cadre is all that comprises the enterprise, these problems do not apply. The venture should keep the organization lean to take advantage of economies, but there should be little if any need to add personnel after transition to an operating division. The self-contained nature of the venture, with its diverse, built-in capabilities, may be duplicated by a parent division. These represent extraneous functions that may create a problem.

Financial Status

Finally, the financial status will carry the most weight in the decision-making process. If cash flow is still negative, a shortsighted divisional manager will find appropriate reasons to use delaying tactics. An upward trend toward a positive flow might be sufficient to convince the manager that he should move. The key question is, when should such consideration of an administrative disposition occur? The preferred time is when cash flow is positive. ROI might also be involved. If the ROI for a previous twelve-month period is positive, acceptance of the venture business is assured. Other yardsticks can be used, but in conjunction with ROI and cash flow, two specific determinants are most helpful. Sales growth and profit growth can indicate when to determine disposition and measure the value of the business to the potential receiving operation. For example, if sales growth has been on target for two years, within perhaps a 10 percent deviation, that substantiates the business and its plans. The time to act would seem imminent, except that it is not so simple since it is advisable that a positive cash flow and ROI accompany this growth. Profit growth may lag behind sales, and there may be no profit the first year or so. Therefore, a one-year on-target profit picture preceded by minimal and expected losses would suffice. Profits are needed for a positive cash flow and a positive ROI. Therefore, a time that meets these criteria can be predetermined from the financial projections. It seems reasonable that two to three years after venture commercialization would be an appropriate time. This can differ greatly in specific businesses, but longer time schedules would become suspect without extreme justification.

Alternative Options

Alternative actions for reassigning a new business go beyond the divisional takeover. While this is a primary alternative in a large company, it may not be valid for smaller ones. Another alternative, as mentioned in the preceding discussion, is to retain autonomy and become an independent division. This should only be considered if the early success is outstanding, independence is compatible with some specific corporate objectives, or the business is obviously large enough to function as an individual profit center. In addition, there is the possibility of combining this enterprise with other new businesses growing from New Venture Methodology. By the same token, although seemingly much less desirable, the business might be fragmented by placing portions such as manufacturing and marketing under some other centralized, specialized operations.

Another possibility to consider is using the business as a base or foundation for additional growth. In that case the new business would continuously be expanded by a constant influx of new products, new parallel lines, and new, smaller, venture-induced businesses.

As a final option, one can spin off the business. Finding a mechanism to do the job is critical. Unless a programmed approach is designed, this will not succeed. Success in this case means producing a reasonable profit. Haphazard spinoffs can cause substantial loss. For this reason the task should be assigned to a separate corporate entity. It should be handled at the highest possible corporate level. The people running the venture business should not be responsible for any transactions, and preferably should not even be involved or informed. The general manager and his key assistant will be required to help by supplying information for the package. If venture people are part of the proposed spinoff, very special precautions and arrangements are required. This is the second selling job of the venture. The first is to sell management on the proposition to undertake the risk and commit funds; the second is to sell the venture to a prospective purchaser. Some problems that will need attention include the timing, to be sure the historical–financial picture is attractive; the price, which must be acceptable to the buyer and profitable to the seller; the identification of a potential purchaser; and the time limit on achieving the goal. If it is not salable, an alternate plan should be ready. All these provide added incentives to assign the task to a corporate staff group who would make it their primary objective.

Some aspects of selling the venture are not immediately evident from the above remarks. Why would one wish to sell the well-founded, solidly grounded new business? Profit is one answer; but it may be a mechanism to obtain new funds for more venturing as well. Since capital is not without limits, many potential ventures may lie fallow owing to a previous commitment of available funds. The sale of a business can initiate a cash turnover that will allow exploitation of additional opportunities. There is a similarity between this approach and a venture management service. Venture management entails heavy reliance on internally generated opportunities for new business, nurtured and developed using New Venture Methodology. This would indicate that new business is developed not only for growth, but to utilize all the internal capabilities of the company to make a profit, even those developed for eventual use by another company.

Sale of the business also demonstrates the productivity of the venture function. This serves as a constant reminder to corporate managers that they are getting their money's worth. It also controls the value of the venture and the venture approach. When sale is contemplated, a real value must be placed on the business. This affords everyone a view of its present worth that might otherwise escape notice. Selling, of course, separates the venture business from other, current operations. It effectively determines an end point and signals the termination of peripheral and supporting efforts. It removes a diluting influence, if one regards a new and apparently successful business as a burden. This might be true in some cases, because of some sudden change in a corporate position.

It might be a bit more dramatic and unusual to consider selling it internally. If new-ventures groups are budgeted by corporate funds, some operating divisions tend to view them with a jaundiced eye. They appear as a drain, a burden, a cost unwillingly accepted. If the venture group becomes self-supporting in the sense that the businesses it develops produce funds for their own use, the venture function holds a stronger position. The division prepared to inherit the business is now asked to pay a fair price. These are the proverbial Chinese dollars that change hands within the company, but they can be a real reserve set aside for funding future venture commercializations. In reality, when a good and desirable business is wanted by two or more operating profit centers, they can bid for it. This is an advantage, since it makes the relative value even more visible and helps support the premise that venturing does work. One could even imagine that a business assigned to a division is a trade-off for technical development means. In exchange for a business, the division would agree to follow specific developmental programs requested by the venture group to find other new venture possibilities. Since new-ventures operations should not do their own research and development and rely on others to supply the developments, some imposed guidance might be increasingly effective. This is the reason for suggesting the trade-off approach. Some of the suggestions made here are nascent, few have been tried. Within certain companies, some might be impractical. But if your thoughts are stimulated and growth goals are achieved, the benefits need no further promoting.

Contribution by Ventures

Measuring the contribution a venture makes to the corporation is a good yardstick for evaluating New Venture Methodology. This is not easily done when there are few ventures started or before some reach maturity. The initial steps to monitoring performance can begin when the venture starts. A chart showing sales, expenses, income, in-

Figure 46. Contribution to corporate sales growth.

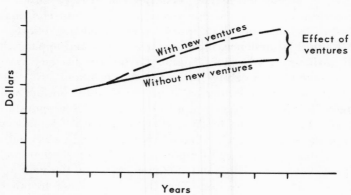

Figure 47. Contribution to profit growth.

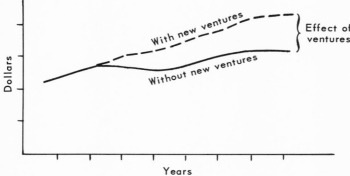

vestment, and ROI can be set up. This would contain the yearly information for each venture on one page if desirable. To complement this chart, a list of ventures showing starting date, previous development costs, and the sales potential at ten years out would be kept. A natural extension of this list is a table showing the venture, its disposition, present and potential sales, investment, and cumulative profit contribution (before or after taxes).

From the collection of data in each preceding document, a graph of dollar sales with time can be prepared showing a curve for forecast sales on the same graph. The value of a sales performance curve is to judge the accuracy of prediction and the growth of the business. If this is done for each venture under way or otherwise disposed of, a composite sales curve for all the ventures can be drawn. The difference between the actual sales performance and that projected or forecast will show the need for other ventures to help reach growth goals or the success achieved with the present ventures.

The important review of contribution to the corporate sales picture is an outgrowth of the venture graphs. By plotting the historical sales performance and extrapolating it into the future, projected growth is revealed. The future sales can be the summation of sales projections for present businesses not resulting from venturing. If a separate line is drawn on the graph, adding to the projected sales from the ventures, the effect appears as shown in Figure 46. More important than sales growth is profit contribution. The same technique is applied. Figure 47 indicates the profit contribution of the ventures. As time progresses, some of the ventures become mature businesses, but they can be separated from other businesses for purposes of evaluating the contribution of new ventures to the company. Properly used,

New Venture Methodology can make the increase substantial and can result in significant contribution.

New Venture Methodology must be pragmatic. When it becomes too involved to function in your company, modifications should be made. The object is to save time and money and to lower risk. It should take advantage of internal expertise and developments. It requires commitment by all, especially upper management. While flexibility is necessary, unidirectionality and a self-contained, multidisciplinary program are critical to success. For ventures to succeed, they must produce businesses that make a profit. New Venture Methodology is a better way to achieve that end.

Appendix
Policy Manual Index

193

Bibliography

Adams, R. M., "An Approach to New Business Ventures," *Research Management,* July 1969.

Anderson, S. L., "Venture Analysis, a Flexible Planning Tool," *Chemical Engineering Progress,* March 1961.

Argenti, John, *Corporate Planning: A Practical Guide.* Homewood, Ill.: Dow Jones-Irwin, 1969.

Benson, George, "Improving the Effectiveness of New Product Development," *Marquette Business Review,* Winter 1971.

Branch, M. C., *The Corporate Planning Process.* AMA, 1962.

Collier, J. R., *Effective Long-Range Business Planning.* Englewood Cliffs, N.J.: Prentice-Hall, 1968.

Crissy, William, and Boewadt, Robert, "Pricing in Perspective," *Sales Management,* June 1971.

Dodge, H. R., *Industrial Marketing.* New York: McGraw-Hill Book Company, 1970.

Edelman, Franz, and Greenberg, J. S., "Venture Analysis: The Assessment of Uncertainty and Risk," *Financial Executive,* August 1969.

Ewing, D. W., *The Human Side of Planning.* New York: The Macmillan Company, 1969.

Ewing, D. W., *The Practice of Planning.* New York: Harper & Row, 1968.

Ewing, D. W. (ed.), *Long-Range Planning for Management.* New York: Harper & Row, 1964.

Ferrell, R. W., *Customer-Oriented Planning.* AMA, 1964.

Fuchs, G. J., and Thompson, G. C., "Management of New-Product Development," *Business Record,* October 1960.

Fulmer, R. M. (ed.), *Organization for New-Product Development.* New York: National Industrial Conference Board, 1966.

Gross, Walter, "An Analytical Approach to Market Forecasting," *Georgia Business,* November 1970.

Hanan, Mack, "Corporate Growth Through Venture Management," *Harvard Business Review,* January–February 1969.

Hertz, D. B., "Risk Analysis in Capital Investment," *Harvard Business Review,* January–February 1964.

Honn, F. J., "New Venture Management," *Commercial Development Journal,* November 1969.

Lanitis, Tony, "How to Generate New Product Ideas," *Journal of Advertising Research,* June 1970.

Lawrence, P. R., and Lorsch, J. W., "New Management Job: The Integrator," *Harvard Business Review,* November–December 1967.

Marquis, D. G., "The Anatomy of Successful Innovations," *Innovation,* No. 7, 1969.

Marting, Elizabeth (ed.), *The Marketing Job.* AMA, 1968.

Marting, Elizabeth (ed.), *New Products, New Profits.* AMA, 1970.

Miller, Ben, *Managing Innovation for Growth and Profit.* Homewood, Ill.: Dow Jones-Irwin, 1970.

Moreno, I. G., *Top Management Long-Range Planning.* New York: Vantage Press, 1963.

O'Dell, W. F., *The Marketing Decision.* AMA, 1968.

Payne, Bruce, *Planning for Company Growth.* New York: McGraw-Hill Book Company, 1963.

Pessemier, E. A., *New Product Decisions, an Analytical Approach.* New York: McGraw-Hill Book Company, 1966.

Peterson, R. W., "New Venture Management in a Large Company," *Harvard Business Review,* May–June 1967.

Ringbakk, K. A., "Why Planning Fails," *European Business,* Spring 1971.

Rudwick, B. H., *Systems Analysis for Effective Planning.* New York: John Wiley & Sons, 1969.

St. Thomas, C. E., *Practical Business Planning.* AMA, 1965.

Schmookler, J., *Invention and Economic Growth.* Cambridge, Mass.: Harvard University Press, 1966.

Scott, B. W., *Long-Range Planning in American Industry.* AMA, 1965.

Springborn, R. C., "New Ventures at W. R. Grace and Company," *Research Management,* July 1969.

Starczewski, J., "How to Seek New Ventures," *Hydrocarbon Processing,* December 1969.

Steiner, G. A., *Top Management Planning.* New York: The Macmillan Company, 1969.

Steiner, G. A., and Cannon, W. M. (eds.), *Multinational Corporate Planning.* New York: The Macmillan Company, 1966.

Stemp, Isay (ed.), *Corporate Growth Strategies.* AMA, 1970.

Uman, D. B., *New Product Programs: Their Planning and Control.* AMA, 1969.

Wallace, R. T., "New Venture Management at Owens-Illinois," *Research Management,* July 1969.

Wallenstein, G. D., *Concept and Practice of Product Planning.* AMA, 1968.

Warren, E. K., *Long-Range Planning: the Executive Vewpoint.* Englewood Cliffs, N.J.: Prentice-Hall, 1966.

West, Raymond, "How to Plan for New Product Development," *Business Management,* September 1970.

Westfall, S. L., "Stimulating Corporate Entrepreneurship in U.S. Industry," *Academy of Management Journal,* June 1969.

Index